9-11

TERROR
IN
AMERICA

by
David Bresnahan

WINDSOR HOUSE
PUBLISHING GROUP INC.

Windsor House Publishing Group
Waxahachie, Texas

9-11 Terror In America

PRINTING HISTORY
First Edition October 2001

ISBN: 188163695X
Library of Congress Card Number: Pending

For information Address:
Windsor House Publishing Group, Inc.
1614 Hill Lane
Waxahachie, Texas 75165

The name "Windsor House" and the logo are trademarks belonging to
Windsor House Publishing Group, Inc.

PRINTED IN THE UNITED STATES OF AMERICA
10 9 8 7 6 5 4 3 2 1

CONTENTS

DEDICATION

Hundreds, even thousands, of heroes were there on September 11, 2001. But many, many other heroes, created by that day's events, have been overlooked in too many reports and commentaries. These are the children of the rescue workers and others who perished in the aftermath of the attacks.

At first these children prayed and clung to hope, but gradually they have been forced to lay hope aside and give in to reality. Mommy or Daddy will not be coming home.

Some are the children of firemen who rushed into burning buildings, knowing their lives would be in peril. These brave men and women put aside thoughts of their own safety and welfare because their hearts were filled with compassion for the thousands who were in grave danger.

Some are the children of passengers on board United Airlines flight 93, whose gallant struggle saved the lives of countless others had the terrorists' intended target had been reached.

Some are the children of nameless and unknown heroes who helped lead others to safety from the towers and buildings in the World Trade Center complex. They guided people down stairwells, made sure everyone got out of offices, and helped to calm those who would have been paralyzed by fear.

Some are the children of heroes in the Pentagon who helped injured and trapped people get to safety, risking their own lives to save others. National security restrictions prevented full media coverage of this crash and rescue effort, thereby minimized public attention, but heroes were there nonetheless.

"This is my commandment, That ye love one another, as I have loved you. Greater love hath no man than this, that a man lay down his life for his friends. Ye are my friends, if ye do whatsoever I command you." (John 15:12-14)

The loss of a parent is always tragic, but the trend of recent decades of more and more divorce and single-parent homes makes it even more challenging. Many families involved in this tragedy were already fragmented in some way. Many children were already wounded by the heartbreak of divorce.

Yet so many parents, like modern heroic knights defending civilization, rode into the battle and saved thousands from near-certain death. Their sacrifices kept thousands of families intact.

But many of these heroes not only gave their own lives, but also forever changed the lives of their own children. They sacrificed their own family's happiness to save happiness for others.

Hundreds of young widows will now be raising their children alone, without the guiding hand of a loving father. And yes, there were women who gave their lives as well, many of whom were single parents. Their children are now orphaned.

Relief agencies are coming to their aid. Churches, the Red Cross, the United Way, and other charitable groups are giving initial help. Grief counselors have their hands full as they try to help those families who for this and every future Thanksgiving will have an empty chair at their celebrations and an empty place in their hearts.

The children of these fallen heroes must now themselves become heroes. They must find ways to become the person of their lost mother's or father's dreams. It will be doubly difficult, but they can do it if they remain strong, courageous, and determined.

Some will be tempted to take an easy path – to give up on life, become bitter and filled with hate. It will be challenging to become stronger, bear each other's burdens, and accomplish the great things their lost parent would have encouraged them to do. The harder path to inner strength and goodness is the path that will take them to the light.

God did not cause this tragedy to happen, nor did He let it happen. The greatest gift God has given us is our free agency to choose our own path in life. God never forces us. We are free to choose for ourselves.

Unfortunately, some choose evil instead of good. Those who choose evil often inflict harm on others because of their evil acts. Those of us impacted by their actions are then faced with the challenge of how to handle what has happened.

We must not blame God. It is God to whom we must turn to deal with the grief of this terrible event. He is a loving God waiting with outstretched arms ready to console us. Life is a trying time. It is a time when we show our faith in God by how we behave. If we love Him, we will live according to His teachings. We do so of our own free will, not by force or because we are compelled.

"And they brought unto him also infants, that he would touch them; but when his disciples saw it, they rebuked them. But Jesus called them unto him, and said, Suffer little children to come unto me, and forbid them not: for of such is the kingdom of God. Verily I say unto you, Whosoever shall not receive the kingdom of God as a little child shall in no wise enter therein." (Luke 18:15-17)

We can reach out to the children of those who have died. We can provide strength through love and our own example. We can be a friend, a guide, a mentor. Remaining family members will need our compassion and support as they keep their family together and work diligently to do the things their fallen father or mother would want them to do. No one can take the place of a missing parent, but we can bring love and strength to help them deal with the void.

The challenges will be many. Sadness will always be there at those special times. The first Christmas season is likely to be most difficult, as will birthdays, ball games, and other events once shared with the now-absent parent. Children going through their teenage years without the loving-but-firm guidance of a father will be at great risk.

We can reach out in many ways, but in the end the children themselves must become heroes. They must now live the lives their fallen parent wanted for them in spite of the challenges they face. They must become stronger and stronger. Rather than let this tragedy destroy them they must draw strength from what happened and succeed.

This will be hard. The battles and challenges they face will be many, and they need to take them on one day at a time. They will stumble and fall. But with the help and loving kindness of neighbors, friends and remaining family they can regain the strength to get back up and keep going.

These children need to know that they have the potential to become heroes. The blood of a hero pulses in their veins, and within them beats a hero's heart. And the light of love and goodness they remember seeing in a now-absent parent's eyes was the light of a Heavenly Father shining through. The Heavenly Father is right here, right now, whenever they turn to Him, for they are truly a Child of God.

Many rescue workers, facing overwhelming shock and grief, turned to God for strength. They, like their fallen comrades, had great faith that helped them at the time of greatest tribulation.

Bereft of the love, faith, and guidance of their lost parent, these young children will struggle throughout life unless they are helped by those who remain to gain a strong faith in God. Such faith strengthened their fallen parent, and it is that faith that will save them as well.

We can all help in a variety of ways. Some can provide a direct one-on-one relationship with a young life shattered by grief. Others can help at a distance through the helping hand of donations and prayers. These things and more can bring strength and hope to deal with life's challenges.

A portion of the proceeds from the sale of this book will be used to help the families of those heroes who are paid far less than they deserve. Many thousands died in this tragedy, but many more thousands lived because of the bravery of a noble group of firefighters and police officers.

Those who purchase this book are helping the families of these heroes, particularly the children who must be heroes every day. We can do more by remembering them in our prayers, donating to other funds and services, and those close enough can reach out to them in a more personal way.

This book is gratefully dedicated to all the heroes in this tragedy – those who died and those who carry on. It is more particularly dedicated to the children who must find strength every day to become all that they can be.

May God bless them all, and may God bless America.

ACKNOWLEDGMENT

This book exists because of Bill Bresnahan, who allowed his personal story to be told. He spent many hours subjecting himself to probing interviews to enable us all to see through his observant veteran policeman's eyes the events following the terrible attack on the U.S. and the world community on September 11, 2001.

Bill's story is heart-touching and eye-opening, giving us all a much more accurate perception of what it was like to be a rescue worker at Ground Zero in those first 24 hours after the attack. Although he does not wish to be called a hero, he indeed is. He exemplifies the many other heroes who were there doing their best to help save a life. We can all be grateful that his story has now been told, for it enables each of us to understand the hundreds of other heroes just like him.

Bill Bresnahan also made it possible to interview the others in this book. Each of them generously shared what is a very personal experience in an effort to help establish this historical record. Each is a hero. Each is an example of the heroism this event brought forth from so many others during those first 24 hours.

And so a very special "thank you" goes to George Sleigh, William Cahill, Timothy Hubbard, James Fenn, Maurice Ottolia, Brian Bliss, and Pat O'Flaherty. Each played an important role, and by sharing their stories they have given us a more complete picture of the monumental task that they and so many others rose to the challenge to perform. Part of that picture comes, too, from the photographs taken by Bill Bresnahan and William Cahill that they generously gave permission to use in this book, and for which they deserve gratitude.

Grateful acknowledgment goes to Lowell Ponte, former *Reader's Digest* Roving Editor, an artist with words whose expert editing skillfully polished this work.

Dwight Wallington and his excellent staff at Windsor House Publishing Group are particularly wonderful and patient. They, too, wanted to make sure this emotional labor of love would be the best we could possibly make it in such a short time. A special thanks to Ken Booster with additional thanks to the typesetter, Ann Carter Lang, and the various printers and binders who were patient with delays and then worked tirelessly to help make this book available so quickly.

David Bresnahan would also like to acknowledge the patience and understanding of his wife and young children, who endured the long weeks without him while this book was being completed.

Bill Bresnahan would also like to acknowledge his wife, his father, his mother, and family. He is also appreciative of all the members of the Philadelphia Police Force with whom he served over the years, and all peace officers everywhere.

Most especially, all who are associated with this book acknowledge the need to thank God. We acknowledge the many blessings that have come in spite of this disaster, and we acknowledge His guidance in the completion of this project.

May God bless America, and may God bless us all.

FOREWORD
By Ben Kinchlow

Tuesday, September 11th ("9-11"), approximately 8:30 on an East Coast morning. An ordinary day. Beautiful by New York standards. Not a hint of what was to come.

8:48 A.M. The unthinkable occurs. An American airliner, with crew and passengers aboard and manned by terrorists, slams into the north tower of the World Trade Center.

Shortly thereafter, another jetliner, with crew and passengers, crashes at full speed into the south tower. Thus begins a day of horror unparalleled in American history, causing grief, revulsion, and justifiable anger.

This book contains eyewitness accounts of a man who survived and others who arrived at Ground Zero just minutes after the horror of that day began to aid in the rescue work.

The tragic truth is, such horror is not unique to mankind. "Man's inhumanity to man" is legendary, and is recorded by history's many muted screams of agonized protest.

What was unique was the method the murderers used to convey their message of hate. Do not be deceived. These men, regardless of the motives attributed to them by their spokesmen or others, are mass murderers. Their actions cannot be justified by any standard of civilized behavior. Their goal was not liberation, or an act of war, or even retaliation for crimes against them. It was murder– pure and simple.

Being an accessory to murder is as much a crime as murder itself. Those who aid and abet the actual deed are as guilty as those who commit the act. Those who planned and financed, and who knowingly housed, provided travel for, or otherwise offered comfort or assistance are just as guilty as those who died with their victims.

Much will be made of their religious convictions. Unfortunately, many of the commentators know little, and comprehend even less, about such matters. People must be clear in their understanding and exact in their approach. No major orthodox religion professes or approves the kinds of anti-human acts perpetrated by these mass murderers. Consequently, no single religion or entire group of people should be held accountable for the actions of a few lawless individuals.

If the acts of September 11th by a small band of individuals by their own free will were wrong, then every human being who opposes what they did should: (1) condemn these acts publicly and (2) provide all possible assistance and support to bring those responsible to justice. It is, therefore, incumbent upon the leadership, the teachers, the adherents, the worldwide Muslim population, and any supporters of Islam to come forth boldly, without reticence or reservation, and unconditionally condemn the acts of these mass murderers. A failure to do so could be construed by some as an overt, or tacit, endorsement of these murders.

As you review the results of the horrific events of this date, please consider two points:

(1) Separate anger from hatred. Righteous indignation and white-hot anger are normal, healthy, justifiable emotions. Anger is, in fact, for those who believe the Bible, supported by Scripture: *"Be angry, but do not sin."* (Ephesians 4:26) For those who would inaccurately portray the Lord Jesus Christ as a pacifist, let us recall it was this same Jesus who, with a scourge, cleansed the temple. His caution was against anger *"without a cause."* (Matthew 5:22) Hatred is not justifiable and, in fact, he who hates is, like those responsible for thousands of deaths, a *"murderer."* 1 John 3:15) Let us allow for righteous anger and a desire for justice, but do not allow hatred for anyone, even the perpetrators, to become a part of our lives. Expend any measure of hatred solely on the actions of those who should be brought speedily to justice.

(2) Separate vengeance from justice. As individuals, we should not be involved in, nor seek to perpetrate, individual acts of vengeance. Vengeance is the rightful province of the Almighty – *"Vengeance is mine, I will repay."* (Romans 12:19) Justice, however, is in the province of man – the duty of duly authorized governments, those appointed to carry out justice. The sentence is clear, *"Whoever sheds the blood of man, by man shall his blood be shed."* (Genesis 9:6) It is morally correct and Biblically supported that the United States should seek to bring to justice, and execute, those who have violated the most sacred of all human rights . . . *the right to life.* Those who violate this law remove from themselves their own right to life. They act with full

knowledge that murder is punishable by death in almost every ordered society. Furthermore, they act of their own free will under no compulsion (save those known only to themselves). The Almighty gives commandments, but He, in no religion known to me, compels or coerces. Every adherent is free to regard or disregard those commandments.

As we review and reflect upon the events chronicled in the pages of this book, let us examine our own motives. Let us recognize our rights to be secure in our persons, to live free from such terrors, and to anticipate and expect that those who violate these rights will be punished.

This book is not about the murderers or their religious principles, nor about the search for justice. This is a book about heroism and horror. It's a book about prayer and effort. This is a book about people whose lives have been scarred by the knowledge of unspeakable horror, but whose scars are soothed by the balm of watching heroes in action. Stand in the choking dust. Sift through the ruins. Listen intently for cries for help. Pray with these men.

Then –

Pray that our leaders will act with wisdom, courage, and boldness. Pray for the comfort and solace of those who grieve. Pray for speedy resolution and swift justice.

Pray.

Minister, broadcaster, author and businessman – Ben Kinchlow is known throughout the world as the longtime co-host of The 700 Club, *and host on the international edition of* The 700 Club, *which was seen in more than 80 countries. He is also a black conservative, Republican, United States Air Force veteran, recipient of the American Legion Award of Merit, and Distinguished Alumnus of Phi Theta Kappa.*

He is the president and founder of Ben Kinchlow Ministries and is actively involved in children's organizations and efforts to eliminate poverty. Kinchlow is the author of two books: Plain Bread *and* You Don't Have To If You Don't Want To. *He maintains a website at www.therealamerica.tv. He is married to the former Vivian Carolyn Jordan. They have three sons and six grandchildren.*

PREFACE

*Not **If**, but **When***

My wife had that look that told me something was very wrong. She struggled to control her emotions as she told me, "You better come see what's happened."

The very moment I saw the images of smoke coming from the north tower of the World Trade Center I thought, "They've really done it." The first thing that came to my mind was terrorism. I remembered a discussion I had with Sen. Robert Bennett (R.-Utah) on New Year's Eve of Y2K. He was at the Emergency Management Center in the State Capital where we were all waiting to see if computer systems everywhere would melt down.

The night passed. The sun rose. Nothing went wrong. Journalists were quickly trying to find something to write about when the only story was that there was no story. Bennett and I discussed the threat of terrorism and some of the training and drills going on with many government agencies.

"It's not a matter of if, it's a matter of when," he told me in a very serious tone. He also said he knew that a number of attempts to attack us had already been prevented, but that sooner or later a group of terrorists would succeed and do something really bad.

His comments came as no surprise. The threat of terrorism using weapons of mass destruction was already known to me. As a reporter I had done investigative articles about not only the potential threat but also the preparations being made by the military and other government agencies.

... as many as 100 small, portable nuclear bombs are missing ...

On September 30, 1998, I reported on Osama bin Laden's deadly plans to attack the United States. I was criticized for doing this and labeled an alarmist. A former CIA employee who knew I was working on terrorism threats called to say he had a fax I should see.

"It was sent by Osama bin Laden to his soldiers all over the world. He's giving them their marching orders. You'll want to see this," he said. "I'm giving this to a few good reporters. Do you want me to fax it to you?"

Naturally I wanted it, but when I told my publisher about it he was unhappy. My source needed protection and could not be revealed. He had been reliable and would be needed for future stories. Giving his name would hurt his business and would certainly eliminate him as a potential future source.

After newspapers in London and Jerusalem came out with stories about the fax, he let me include information about it buried in another article. Two days later my publisher agreed to let me mention the fax in a somewhat related story.

When I spoke to official sources from the FBI regarding the threat posed by Osama bin Laden, I was told that this millionaire Saudi Svengali was regarded as a madman with a bark bigger than his bite. The FBI did not want a copy of my fax and would not say if they had already seen it. They told me bin Laden was incapable of carrying out the goals of the fax.

The fax was purportedly intercepted as it went to 5,000 or more "soldiers" stationed in groups or "cells" all around the world, including some within the U.S. The translation of the apparently Arabic writing on the fax was written in between the lines by someone. It never told his "soldiers" what specific targets to attack, but it stated goals for attacks on U.S. interests. The fax did not say how to accomplish the goals, nor did it specify a day or hour to strike.

According to the fax, the attacks should:
• Bring commercial airlines to a halt
• Stop all maritime traffic
• Occupy U.S. embassies around the world
• Shut down U.S. banking

Three years later bin Laden appears on his way to accomplishing his goals, despite the assurance of intelligence sources at the time of his fax that this was impossible.

For the first time in history, every commercial flight in the U.S. has been grounded, as have many international flights. The financial markets were all closed, and there has been a major decline as well as storm warnings of increased unemployment and recession.

Will an attack on shipping be next? What about our embassies?

The terrorists use fear as a weapon, knowing it can be contagious.

All those I interviewed for this book said they expect future attacks on U.S. soil. Polls show that a majority of Americans also believe that more attacks are coming. People are preparing for emergencies by acquiring things far beyond extra food and water for 72-hour survival kits. One week after the attacks of September 11th, a survey found that military surplus gas masks cannot be purchased at any price. All inventories were exhausted within days of the attacks.

My intelligence sources have told me for several years that we are under a very real threat of attacks by terrorists using weapons of mass destruction. These attacks, they expect, will come sooner or later – without warning. We are also being targeted by relentless cyber attacks that could disrupt computer systems that are the central nervous system of our telephones, financial transactions, and Internet communications worldwide. Such attacks can kill our computer systems in much the same way nerve gas kills people.

I am not the only journalist to report that as many as 100 small, portable nuclear bombs are missing from what had been the arsenal of the Soviet Union. These superweapons are sometimes called suitcase A-bombs because they are so portable. They can be placed at a target location and detonated by remote control using as their "delivery system" a terrorist with a small private airplane, fishing boat, or ordinary automobile. Even the writers at Disney called me to get information about the missing bombs because they have been planning a movie about a terrorist attack using such a device.

Other possible attacks include the use of chemical and biological weapons that can be sprayed in the air or placed in our water supplies, or destruction of key power plants and communication systems. Bin Laden's forces could easily accomplish most if not all such goals. What once seemed to the ravings of a madman are now stark and real dangers.

This is why I felt no surprise when images of the first attack on the World Trade Center tower appeared on television. It was a shock, but no surprise. This was, I knew instantly, the work of a terrorist group. Then suddenly the second plane hit, and my shock turned to anger that we failed to prevent this horrible tragedy.

But then, just as suddenly, my thoughts turned to what must be going on at what soon we soon would call "Ground Zero." The pictures on television were not bringing us the horror that must certainly be taking place around, and even more so inside, those towers. In my mind I was trying to visualize the death and destruction that had already taken place, along with the panic of those left alive. My thoughts: "What must it be like? What about the people in the towers above and below the floors where the plane hit? Will they get out?" I didn't like the probable answers.

Little did I know that my cousin Bill Bresnahan was at that same time listening to the news and making a decision to go and help. I should have known he would react that way. He was highly decorated for acts of bravery during his years as a Philadelphia police officer and SWAT team member. He was a hero who almost lost his life fighting bad guys. His permanent disabilities forced him into early retirement.

The call went out for help, and Bresnahan was quick to respond. He was not the only one. Other police and firefighters within reach of New York also sped to the scene. They knew help would be urgently needed, and they were ready and willing to do whatever was asked of them.

This book is an effort to give some perspective to this horrific tragedy by seeing it through the eyes of people who were right there at Ground Zero in the first 24 hours. During that time most of us only saw what television was able to show us. The media was not allowed in, and because of that what we learned from it was limited.

. . . bin Laden appears on his way to accomplishing his goals . . .

We can get no closer than to hear personally from the last survivor to escape from one of the towers. George Sleigh actually watched out his 91st floor window as the first plane slammed into the building just a few feet above him. His story of how he got all his workers down the stairs and out just as the first tower collapsed is dramatic and inspirational.

As Sleigh was racing down the stairs in an hour-long struggle to escape, firefighters were rushing in. More than 300 police and firemen gave their lives in a valiant effort to save other lives. The stories of what they did will touch your heart, remind you how precious life is, and deepen your awareness of the selfless goodness of these heroes.

Bresnahan and each of the rescue workers interviewed in this book offer perspective to those of us who were there in our hearts and prayers but not physically to see and experience for ourselves. But just as they provide perspective to us, we have a perspective and knowledge base they did not have.

Watching on television gave most of us the 'big picture,' the overall view of the situation and what was going on. Those like George Sleigh had no idea what was happening beyond their own very confined surroundings. Many of the rescue workers describe events, but could not give details except about what they personally observed.

And so this book contains the impressions and experiences of a number of people involved in this enormous tragedy. It makes no attempt to provide details beyond what was seen through the senses of those who were there.

If this were a news article, I as a reporter would attempt to bring together information from various sources and combine that with timelines and other information resources to provide detailed explanations and factual data. This book instead records the actual words and experiences of those involved – their perceptions of what was going on around them, their feelings, and their reactions.

When a rescuer, for example, describes various buildings there is no attempt to identify the specific building. The rescuers all expressed confusion about their locations and the names of specific buildings and streets. They also were unable to identify many other workers they spent time with. They worked together as brothers without even knowing each other's names. Strangers came from other states and found themselves working next to buildings they couldn't identify. And when a few survivors were found alive, the rescuers were filled with joy even though they did not know so much as the name of the person who is alive today because of them.

As a journalist I could add to their knowledge about such details. Instead I decided to let them tell their own stories in their own voices. After all the interviews, it became obvious that plenty of news reports have documented the hard, cold facts.

This book instead lets these soft, warm human beings who lived through the horrible events have their say. Most are telling their stories publicly for the first time. And through them you can touch some of what they experienced, mind to mind and heart to heart.

They did not come to me to tell their story. I had to seek out each of them and ask for their help with this project. Not one of them had any desire to be seen as a hero or someone special. They wanted to go on with life with no special attention to what they did during this event. Each had to be convinced that his story represented many other stories that the American people, indeed the people of the world, needed to know in order to understand more fully what happened and what it was like during those first 24 hours at Ground Zero.

In my effort to tell the story of the experiences at Ground Zero I am in no way minimizing what happened at the Pentagon or at the crash site in Pennsylvania. Perhaps witnesses to those events will make themselves known to me so their stories can be told as well.

The proceeds of this book, I am pleased to say, will go to The Hero Fund, established by the Grand Council of the United Emerald Societies, a national organization to which many of the fallen rescue workers belonged. The Hero Fund will benefit the families of rescue workers who lost their lives, as well as those who lived and now bear the scars of this experience. We have their assurance that they will use these funds to help the families of both firefighters and police officers impacted by this event, whether they are members of the Emerald Society or not.

My life has been forever changed by interviewing the people for this book. They enabled me to see, hear, and experience a part of what it was like for them to deal with this attack. Now it is my job to convey this to you so that you also can gain a more human perspective of this event.

. . . he knew that attempts to attack us had already been prevented, but that sooner or later a group of terrorists would succeed.

If, God forbid, more such attacks are to come, then what we can learn from those who tell their stories here may be key to our survival, both as individuals and as a nation. Theirs are the qualities of intelligence, courage, compassion, cooperation, determination, and love that made them survivors – or willing to make sacrifices so others could survive. From their personal stories, many of you could become inoculated against the terror with which those such as bin Laden aim to infect America and the world.

As President George W. Bush said, we feel horror at what was done on September 11th, but we should not feel terror. The terrorists use fear as a weapon, knowing it can be contagious. But courage and goodness and love can also spread by example from one person to another, as Someone from Galilee taught. By reading this book, you could "catch" the best virtues of those you will meet in these pages.

Each of them expresses a deep faith in God. They came from a variety of denominations and levels of faith prior to the attacks. Facing Ground Zero, they all turned to God and here share with us some very personal feelings. Men with reputations as big, tough, no nonsense cops were very open about their grief. Some spoke of their already-strong faith and how it sustained them. Others said they had renewed or increased their faith as a result of what happened.

My own faith has been strong for many years, and I am grateful that I know God lives. Jesus is indeed the Christ, the true Son of God. I know that God hears and answers prayer, and I'm grateful for his plan of salvation and the gospel of Jesus Christ.

This tragedy, horrible as it is, has moved many people to seek what has been missing in their lives. I believe that an infinitely larger plan than that of any madman or earthly king is unfolding through what happened 9-11-01.

"It's not a matter of _if_, it's a matter of _when_."
– Senator Robert Bennett (R.-Utah)

CHAPTER 1

Last Man Out?

George Sleigh stood at the 91st floor window of his office in the World Trade Center's north tower and watched as American Airlines Flight 11 crashed into the floors directly above him. There was no time for panic. Sleigh calmly shouted to his fellow employees to get under their desks.

An instant later the ceiling and a wall came crashing in. All the employees, fortunately, were safe beneath their desks – safe, at least, for the moment.

Sleigh and his fellow employees were alive, but Sleigh knew he had to get them out of the building fast. His mind flashed back to 1993, when he helped evacuate people from the 106th floor of the south tower. A terrorist bomb had exploded in its parking structure. If the explosive-laden vehicle had been parked against a key pillar, demolition experts later calculated, its detonation could have toppled the entire tower into Manhattan – killing all inside and thousands more where it fell.

His evacuation down 106 flights of stairs challenged Sleigh in 1993. Now 63, he would have to make that stressful scramble for safety again. Without consciously thinking about it, he sensed that his life depended on going down all those stairs once more.

"My legs hurt for weeks," he said of the experience in 1993, but that memory did not slow him from what he now had to do to save himself and the others in his office.

" . . . survivors escaping down the stairs encountered firemen and rescuers coming up . . . "young guys . . . not even shaving yet . . . that's how young they looked."

Sleigh is a naval architect for American Bureau of Shipping, a company founded in New York City in 1862. The main office is now in Houston, Texas. That day only 12 of the 22 Manhattan employees were in the office. No one else was on the floor because all its other offices were vacant.

Sometimes bad news turns out to be a blessing. ABS's offices used to be on the 106th floor of the other WTC tower, but a budget tightening in late 1999 downsized them to a smaller, less expensive office space on the 91st floor of the north tower. The first plane crashed into the floors just above that 91st floor, narrowly missing Sleigh and his office mates. The second plane hit the south tower and most likely would have trapped or incinerated Sleigh and his co-workers had they remained in that prestigious 106th floor office.

Sleigh had not thought about fate in those moments after the crash. Only after it was over and he agreed to be interviewed from his home in New Jersey did he ponder his good fortune. Had his company not moved, or had the move been to a north tower office higher than the 91st floor, he would almost certainly have died in horror and agony as did thousands of others.

More than luck would be needed to get him out alive on September 11, 2001. Quick action and level heads were essential if Sleigh and his co-workers were to survive. No one then knew that the building would totally collapse in just one hour and 40 minutes. No one knew a second plane was soon to hit the south tower causing that to collapse in just 52 minutes. Few imagined the kind of nightmare that was unfolding. And these great steel and concrete skyscrapers where 50,000 people worked might fill with smoke from a fire, but few suspected that they could shatter into dust and twisted metal. These highest achievements of wealth and technology seemed unsinkable . . . like the Titanic.

Rush to Ground

Sleigh had taken Monday off (the day before the attack) and was just returning to work on Tuesday after a long weekend. He had a large work-load and arrived at 7:30 a.m. Although he had a window office that faced north towards the Empire State Building, Sleigh was too busy catching up on E-mails and phone messages to admire the sunny morning view.

"At the time the plane crashed into the building I was on the phone talking to one of our other offices," said Sleigh, who had turned away from the window while he was working. Forty years earlier he had moved from his native England to find opportunity in America. He has lived here ever since.

"My office was right on the north wall of the building, looking out over the north part of the city. I was on the phone when I heard a loud roar and looked out the window. And here, almost upon us, was a plane. A large passenger plane. It was staring right at the building. It was above us and to my right, so I saw the underbelly of the plane. I noticed that the wheels were up. That kind of registered with me. All of a sudden it hit the building."

Sleigh may be one of only a handful of people who saw the plane from the level of the building where it hit and lived to tell about it. He didn't think anyone else in his office saw it other than perhaps a glimpse just at the last moment. By the time he turned and looked out the window he was only able to see the plane for only a few seconds.

. . . he opened a door, looked into a corridor, and saw flames.

"To estimate, it was two, maybe three plane lengths away at the most when I first saw it. Maybe it was farther away than that, but it was moving at a high speed," he described.

Eyewitnesses on the ground reported that both planes, just before they hit, seemed suddenly to accelerate in the direction of their targets. At least one of the planes reportedly created a sonic boom.

"It didn't seem to be (accelerating), but of course the plane was coming towards me, and most of the sound would be from the back. It didn't sound like it was increasing speed as it came toward the building, but it was so close. The thought hardly registered. Suddenly it was there," Sleigh described.

When he first looked up at the fast-approaching jetliner he felt no sudden panic or fear because he did not think the plane would hit the building.

"My first thought was crazy, but I thought, 'This guy is low.' Sometimes we see planes around the building, but they're quite a bit higher than that. And then it was into the building. I mean, it was that fast. I didn't really have time to think where he might be headed or what he was doing," Sleigh said.

During the few seconds he watched the plane, Sleigh was able to get a good view. Because the plane hit just above the 91st floor where Sleigh was working, he found himself looking at the bottom of the plane. Its right wing hit the floors directly above him. The main body of the plane impacted farther away from Sleigh, towards the middle of the building. Fuel tanks are located in the wings of planes, and these tanks were nearly full because the flight was fueled for a trip all the way to Los Angeles.

"I saw the underside of the front of the plane and one wing. I don't remember seeing an engine. I saw white and blue, and it registered in my mind as a large passenger plane. It wasn't some little two-seater. It was above me and to my right," he described.

He said he believes most if not all the people on the floors above the 91st were killed instantly or trapped when the plane hit. He knows the plane hit extremely close to his location. He believes his survival is a miracle.

"The plane was not flying level, so maybe part of it struck the same level as our floor. (Part of) the plane was above us maybe a couple floors, but where exactly it hit I'm uncertain," Sleigh said.

He had been in a previous terrorist attack on the World Trade Center in 1993, but Sleigh says it never occurred to him that the crash was anything but an accident. His description of what happens next comes from his own perception. He had no access to news reports and knew nothing about the second crash into the south tower until much later. Oddly, he was unaware that the south tower had collapsed, even though its debris nearly killed him.

. . . when the blast occurred and he looked behind him, all he saw was flying debris . . . where the guard had been . . .

"That moment (after the plane hit) was chaotic," Sleigh said. "My cubicle is up against the end partition wall of the office, and that wall kind of crumpled. All the ceiling tiles and the light fixtures came down. Books came off my book shelves. I was buried in that debris. One of my colleagues came rushing along to see if I was okay, and I said, "Yes, I'm all right," and crawled out from under. At that point I looked around. There didn't appear to be any glass broken in our office. The windows were still intact, and from what I could see the structure was still intact. There were no bent beams or anything like that. So we grouped together."

"Because of all the stuff coming down around me, I don't remember actually feeling the building move. I just heard the loud crashing. I didn't feel anything until all of this stuff started to fall down around me," said Sleigh. He says he heard no sound of an explosion during or after the crash.

"After the crash the noise stopped. It was quiet. It was relatively quiet. I couldn't hear any sound of any action going, any explosions, or any such thing as that," he explained.

As his co-workers crawled out from under the debris, they were confused about what happened. Instinct, or perhaps divine inspiration, told Sleigh to get everyone out immediately. The tendency to stand around and talk about what happened would delay their escape. Sleigh had an urgent feeling they needed to get moving.

"I think only two, maybe three people in the office perhaps saw the plane. The rest were elsewhere at that point," he explained. "I just called out, and everyone was saying, 'What happened?' I said, 'Well, a plane has hit the building. Let's get out of here.' We just marshaled our people. We counted heads to make sure everyone who was there was accounted for and headed down the stairs."

The only safe way out of the building was to use the stairwells, not the elevators, as everyone there had been taught. Fortunately more than one set of stairs was near their office. But before they went down Sleigh ducked back inside. He had no thought that the office would be destroyed, but he also had no idea when he would be allowed back in the building.

"In retrospect I was foolish, but my briefcase was in my office buried under the debris. Just before we left I said, 'I need my address book with my phone numbers in it.' It was in my briefcase. So I crawled back in and got that out. I mean that was only 30 seconds. I was in and out like that, and then we headed down the stairs," he explained.

"I just assumed that at some point we'd be able to get back into our office and get important documents and so on. That's the way it was after the bombing in 1993," Sleigh said of his initial expectations. He never thought the building would come down.

"The other tenants on our floor had moved out," explained Sleigh. "There was a dot com company that moved out nine months ago. They had a lot of young people. And there was a space next to us which the Port Authority donated where young artists did artwork, but none were in that day. We were the only tenants on the floor. Some other people did things there from time to time. As far as I know, everyone who was on that floor got out safely."

"I was just blown by an irresistible force. I had to go with it."

Two stairwells could be used to get out. The first one they tried had too much smoke. The next one had some smoke, but not as much. Both stairwells were empty. There were no people coming down from above. The power remained on, so the lights in the stairs were working, but sprinkler systems were activated and water was flowing into the stairs making them hazardous.

Sleigh took up a position at the end of his group so he would know that all members of his group were in front of him all the way down. He didn't want to have anyone fall behind. Just a couple floors below he opened a door, looked into a corridor, and saw flames. The fire from the plane's fuel had now spread downward.

"At one point I guess we were two or three floors lower. We looked down a corridor and we saw flames. They weren't in the stairwell, but we looked out into one of the doorways on one of the floors and noticed flames as we were going down," said Sleigh. He was unable to say exactly which floor he was on when he spotted the fires, but he saw no sign of people on the level that was ablaze.

At first, Sleigh's co-workers were the only people in the stairwell. No one ever joined them from higher floors. Sleigh was the slowest member of the group and eventually lost sight of the others, who moved faster than he did. Although he was moving slowly, no one from a higher floor ever caught up with him.

"We seemed to be the highest floor where people were able to get out of the building, at least so far as I was able to determine. So there was nobody from above. As we went down, obviously people were filtering in from other floors. We just continued on down in that way," he explained.

As he went lower, water from the sprinklers diminished and then disappeared, which indicated that there were no fires on those lower floors. Later, nearer to the bottom, water appeared again.

Sleigh saw no people running in panic, although many were moving quickly. He said that Port Authority building security officers stationed at several places along the way encouraged people along.

"People walked fairly briskly," said Sleigh. "Every few floors Port Authority people were telling us to hold on to the rails because the stairs were a little wet. They didn't want anyone slipping and hurting themselves on the way down. So we proceeded cautiously but as efficiently as we could."

More than halfway down the building – exactly how far he could not say – Sleigh began to encounter firemen coming up the stairs. The stairs were crowded with people trying to escape and firemen trying to go up. He gave no thought to it at the time, but now he realizes that most, if not all, of those firemen perished.

"On the way down we passed a lot of firemen and rescue workers," Sleigh explained. "I had experienced this during the '93 bombing. That explosion was down kind of in the center and affected both towers. The big problem at that time was smoke, a lot of smoke. It forced us to evacuate our floor on that occasion. In '93 we actually just went up on the roof and stayed on the roof until the smoke subsided and we were able to walk down.

"As we were going down the stairway on September 11, firemen were walking up. I felt sorry for those guys, not because I knew their fate but just because of the load they were carrying. They had all the gear with them – 50, 60 pounds of stuff each. Oxygen tanks, axes, and heavy firefighting clothes."

He said it was a struggle for him to go down the stairs. He couldn't imagine how difficult it must be for the firemen to go up the stairs with all their gear. The firemen didn't speak, but he and others tried to offer words of praise and encouragement.

"No, they didn't say anything. We were encouraging them and they were going about doing their job, you know. I guess they were searching floor by floor to make sure everyone was out," Sleigh said.

He never imagined as they passed the firemen that these men were in any unusual danger. Who believed that the entire tower would come down? Even though they were inside the building, their limited perception and lack of information prevented them from knowing how perilous their situation was.

"Only later did the extent of the tragedy sink in – that those guys probably didn't make it out," Sleigh said of the firemen he passed on the stairs. "I mean that was really incredible. A lot of young guys too. Just fresh-faced young guys, 19- or 20-years-old they seemed to be. Yeah, that was disturbing. That thought has haunted me since then. Seeing those people and realizing that they didn't make it."

"I . . . saw what looked like a war zone . . . Horrible things like you might have seen in Beirut."

The trip down from the 91st floor was long and tiring for everyone involved, and it became slower as people from many floors began to reach the bottom, causing a bottleneck.

"As we got near the bottom – and I cannot recall what floors they were – the flow came to a stop a couple of times. With so many people, there was just no movement at all. But there was no panic. Nobody was shouting 'move along!' Everyone just proceeded down the stairs in a very orderly manner, said Sleigh.

Survivors escaping down the stairs encountered firemen and rescuers coming up the stairs. The stairs were crowded near the bottom of the building, which made it difficult for the firemen to squeeze by. Although few words were spoken, Sleigh said he has vivid memories of the young faces he saw.

"I tell you, the ones who impressed me were the young guys. I just recall seeing a lot of these young guys. One of my colleagues who I was walking down with me said, 'These guys are not even shaving yet.' I mean, that's how young they looked.

"They just looked like young, fresh-faced kids, you know? Those are the ones that I remember. They were stoic as they went about their job, you know. They were serious. They weren't laughing. They weren't wise cracking. They were just going about the seriousness of the job that they were doing. They were going up those stairs not knowing what they were going into, and in retrospect they probably never came out," said Sleigh.

"I was reading some of the accounts recently. I mean, they were told at some point to get out. I mean, there's no point to going any further. And maybe some of them did get out, but I know a lot of them didn't. Look at the numbers of the ones who are missing. It's just incredible.

"Everything is quite vivid in my mind. There was never a point where I lost awareness of what was going on and what was going on around me. I think I have pretty good recall of what I went through," said Sleigh.

During the long climb down, the conversations were few, but when needed Sleigh said he did what he could to reassure those who were struggling.

"I was just encouraging everyone," said Sleigh. "A few women were getting, well, not hysterical but distraught. A little distraught. I just tried to encourage them to keep on walking and kept saying, 'We'll get out.' There was one girl, a Japanese girl walking down with her shoes in her hands. I said, 'You better put those shoes on.' The shoes were not very substantial. I don't know what they would have done when she got outside in all of that rubble. I said you should put your shoes on. You don't want to be walking down without them."

The trip down the stairs was not only emotionally trying for some, it was also a physical challenge and a hazard for many. At places the stairs were wet and very slippery. Sleigh reminded people around him to hold the handrail.

"We didn't want anyone falling down and hurting their back and needing to be carried out. We wanted to make sure everyone walked down and walked out of the building,' he said.

Sleigh said he prayed throughout his journey down the stairs. He said his strong Christian faith sustained him and gave him strength. He also prayed for others along the way.

"I have a faith in God that He is Sovereign, and I just prayed. It was his will to spare my life," he explained. "I didn't notice anyone who was praying, but I was praying within my heart. One of the Port Authority people on the stairway directing people, he was very upbeat. He was encouraging every one. He said, 'God has protected you. He'll take care of you.'"

"... I looked down and saw my trousers soaked in blood."

Only 15 minutes after Flight 11 hit Sleigh's building, United Flight 175 sliced through the south tower. Sleigh and the others inside the building who were trying to escape were unaware that this had happened. They still believed the first plane crash was an accident. It never occurred to Sleigh that it was a terrorist attack. He was completely unaware of the attack on the Pentagon, or the crash of United Airlines Flight 93 in Pennsylvania.

"Our group of 11 or 12 had gotten strung out along the way. One other guy was with me most of the way down and then he and I got separated toward the end. We got on to the bottom of the stairwell which is on the mezzanine level of the World Trade Center," said Sleigh.

Port Authority security personnel were at the bottom directing people coming from the stairwells. Sleigh had no way to know if these security people were able to escape.

"They directed us to go one level lower, which is the subterranean concourse level, down an escalator which of course wasn't moving. We walked down, and they directed us through into the concourse," he said.

"The concourse connects all the buildings together. It has a number of stores and various subway stations and the train entrance," he explained.

People were sent to the concourse level to get them away from the building because it was too dangerous to exit the main doors on the mezzanine level. Broken glass and debris were falling from both towers and anyone escaping the building would be at risk of getting hit by that debris. The concourse provided a way for people to get farther away from the towers before exiting into the open.

"Building security people directed us through the concourse and pointed which direction to go. By that time there were 3 or 4 inches of water in the concourse. Sprinklers were going full blast. I was soaked from top to bottom," said Sleigh.

By now the entire crowd of people who came down the stairwells had sped far enough ahead of Sleigh that he no longer saw them. He and just two other men, unknown to him, were the only ones left. A security guard directed them into a side hallway.

"I just got through the first part of the concourse through one of the side sections or hallways when I heard a huge blast – an explosion. (It came) from the direction of building two (south tower). I still haven't determined what that was, whether it was something that preceded the building coming down, or if was just an explosion, or if it was the collapse. It was a loud blast. I looked behind me just over my shoulder as I was walking away and saw these sprinkler jets were now going horizontal and huge amounts of debris were flying through the air. So I just started to run away from that as fast as I could," he said.

The blast came from the direction of the south tower. "I was walking out of the north tower and it came from my right which was the direction of the south tower, which is building two. So whatever was happening in building two, whether it was the collapse of the building, or something that preceded it, I don't know," he said.

"I was walking east through the concourse and I was out of its main section that connected building one (north tower) with building two," he added. "I'm not too totally sure where I was. I was a little disoriented at this point. Between the buildings, if you're on the street level, there's a plaza level. I was walking east. I would have been under the plaza level at the point that this explosion occurred. And the blast seemed to come from my right and behind me. I was not under either of the towers at the time. I was in the central area that was not directly below the towers."

Sleigh knew that all his co-workers were in front of him, and he had never seen a single person overtake him. He doesn't know what happened to the Port Authority security guards who directed him through the concourse, but when the blast occurred and he looked behind him all he saw was flying debris in the place where the guard had been just moments before.

"Suddenly all the lights went out. It was pitch black. Totally black,"said Sleigh. "I stayed on my feet, fortunately. I was just blown by an irresistible force. I had to go with it. It blew me across the concourse. I was by myself at that point. I think we were separated, maybe 20 feet apart going through this thing. There was no one immediately around me.

"I was more or less on my own, and I just, I thought that was the end. I really did. I thought that was the end of my life. I just prayed to God to save me, and He answered my prayer. I ended up against a wall of the concourse and a doorway, which seemed to be quite secure. There was this dense cloud of dust that engulfed us, so I just stood there. Thank God for taking me that far. I just waited. It was totally black. I couldn't see a thing.

<u>Light at the End</u>

"And then as the dust settled I started to see some outlines of things. An overhead light was still burning. One overhead light about five or six feet away. I never saw another one in the whole place. I walked over to it and just started to call out, 'Hello. Hello. Anyone around here?' A couple of guys heard me and came over. Together we started to shout out and see if there was anyone there. Some Port Authority security personnel heard us and told us to walk to them. They had flashlights. We just followed their directions to their lights, and they led us out of the building.

"They took us through, and we came up another level of stairs into building five. From there they took us out into the plaza area and then out into the street.

"I heard a loud roar and looked out the window. And here, almost upon us, was a plane."

"From the level I came out of building five I saw the concourse area. I did not look back at the buildings. For whatever reason, I didn't do that. I just looked across the concourse area and saw what looked like a war zone. Piles of debris here and there were burning. Horrible things like you might have seen in Beirut. The area was covered with piles of debris."

He emerged exhausted from nearly an hour climbing down 91 stories, soaked to the skin by sprinklers, and covered in soot and dust from debris. It was in his eyes, ears, and mouth. He was disoriented and unaware that his leg had been badly cut by debris that hit him down in the concourse. He had no curiosity to look back at the towers. His whole focus was on continuing to walk away from the disaster he had escaped. Without knowing what happened, he had escaped the worst attack ever on U.S. soil.

"I was just covered from head to toe in this stuff. It was incredible. As I was walking out some photographers took some pictures. One of my sons in England called me the next day and said, 'Dad your picture's on the front page of all the London papers here.' I'm the guy carrying the bag," said George Sleigh of his appearance as he emerged from the concourse below the World Trade Center.

"It didn't look like there was a whole lot ahead of me. These two guys I had hooked up with in the building, the three of us were together. We walked out together. I didn't even get their names or anything. We just walked out together, kind of like zombies I guess. There was debris all around and dust everywhere. It was just a mess. Papers. The place was strewn with papers. It was just unbelievable.

"I discovered later that they were taking people out of the building in all different directions. Everybody wasn't coming out of this one exit. By the time we were coming out we were just a few stragglers. I mean, other than the two men I was with I didn't see anyone else left in the building at that point."

"That thought has haunted me . . . Seeing those people and realizing that they didn't make it."

Sleigh later learned that his colleagues had been directed out of the building via a different exit, which prevented them from meeting on the outside. Survivors came down many different stairwells and escaped in all directions around the two towers.

"Small fires were burning everywhere," Sleigh said. "I just continued to walk east, away from the complex up Church Street and then up to Broadway. Somewhere along the way I looked down and saw my trousers soaked in blood. I thought I had twisted my knee or something. My knee hurt, and my left ankle hurt, but I just thought it was probably a sprain. So, I just kept walking to Broadway. A police officer there gave me a bottle of water and told me to wash my eyes and my mouth out, which I did. He saw my leg and said, 'You look like you need some attention.'

"An ambulance was there, but it was full, so he walked me north on Broadway for a block and then flagged down an EMT vehicle coming in and put me in the back. They took me to a hospital. As I was getting into that vehicle the cop shouted to the driver, 'Get out of here! The building is coming down!'"

Sleigh said he does not know if the collapse was the south tower, which came down at 9:55 a.m., or the north tower which came down at 10:28 a.m. He did not watch the collapse and did not see the time as he got into the ambulance. He is confused about what happened while he was in the concourse. He doesn't know if the explosion that nearly killed him was in reality the south tower coming down, or if it was something else. If it was the south tower coming down, then he spent an hour coming down the stairs, which he says seems to be longer than what he estimates.

"That's what I was surmising, but I couldn't say for sure. I wasn't looking at my watch to see what time it was. Whether or not the explosion I experienced was the building coming down, I don't think so. It might have been something that preceded the building coming down.

"It sounded like a definite explosion. It wasn't something crumbling and falling. It was an explosion – a bang. Whether the flames had reached a gas main or something I really don't know," Sleigh said.

"It could be (the collapse of the south tower). It could be. I don't really know. I didn't have that understanding at that point. I didn't know precisely what time it was because I didn't look at my watch until I got to the hospital. I was trying to make a phone call to my wife from the hospital and I looked at my watch. It was then 10:30 A.M., so it was a little before 10:30 when I got to the hospital.

"I haven't any other satisfactory explanation as to what that was. It's hardly conceivable to me that it took us an hour to get out of that building, because in '93 when we came down from the roof it took about 50 minutes. And we were coming down maybe 15 floors fewer than in '93, in a well-lit staircase. I just don't really know," said Sleigh, uncertain about much he had experienced.

"When I got into the ambulance the guy gave me some oxygen and checked my leg. There were a couple of deep cuts in my right leg," he said.

"I started to learn what had happened from the ambulance driver. I hadn't known about the second plane hitting the other building or about the attack on the Pentagon. Up until that time I thought one plane had an accident.

"I was just horrified," said Sleigh "But the enormity of what had taken place didn't grab me until later. When I saw what happened I was just amazed that we were able to leave the building."

"I'm just overwhelmed by the evil force that exists in the world."

"The ambulance guy bandaged me up and I got to the hospital. They made me take a shower outside with all my clothes on, just to get the dust off before I went in. I didn't realize how filthy I was. Get all this dust out of me. Out of my face, and out of my nose, and mouth and ears. That kind of stuff. Then they admitted me to the hospital and put me in a cubicle in the emergency section. I took my shoes and socks off and I noticed I had a very deep cut on my left ankle. It was open to the bone and they cleaned it out, squeezed it together, and stapled it shut," Sleigh described.

Sleigh is convinced that no one from a floor higher than his came out of the north tower. He believes he was the last one out from the highest point in the building.

"From the sound of things, and from what I gathered, I have not read any reports of anyone who was above us. If everyone left as promptly as we did they would have all been out and would have come down the stairs behind us," he explained.

The doctor working on him at the hospital had no time because of the number of injured he was dealing with. He said, "I'm sorry we don't have any time today. Hold your breath." He then stapled the wound shut, but Sleigh did not complain. Later he had to return to another doctor for treatment because the wound became badly infected. It had to be reopened, cleaned out, and sewn up. Instead of complaining Sleigh said he was happy his injuries were so minor.

Sleigh was surprised by how few victims were in the hospital that he could see. And he was also surprised at how quickly he was treated and released.

"I was sent to Beth Israel, which is kind of a second tier that would deal with the casualties. There were quite a few people there, but it wasn't overflowing. I mean, they got me right in and got me a cubicle. I didn't have to wait for somebody to leave. I was done and they signed me out by 11:30 that morning," he said.

". . . the potential is there for more of the same to happen again."

Sleigh never let go of his big canvas carrying case. He said it may have prevented further injury.

"I caught more grief over that. 'Look at this guy. What a loyal guy. He's still got his briefcase.' I don't know. I just hung on to it. Actually, today, it's a canvas bag, and my wife scrubbed it out and we threw it in the washer and it came out good, but I looked at it today and it's got some cuts in it. Maybe it saved me from some additional debris that may have hit me," he said.

Terrorists twice aimed dead-center, intending in 1993 and 2001 to kill its occupants. Sleigh was in their crosshairs during both attacks, but he was not slain.

Despite the tremendous loss of life, destruction of buildings and businesses, and his own suffering, Sleigh says he doesn't hate the terrorists or those who helped them.

"I'm very angry that they did this," he said. "I don't have any hate in my heart towards them. They're driven by a belief that has been ingrained in them from a false belief system, I believe. They're controlled by people with the power and resources to control and motivate them to do such things. So I have no personal hatred towards them. I don't feel that. I'm just very angry that they would bring so much grief and sadness to so many families.

"I certainly don't think it's over. It was certainly very involved, very well planned, and extremely well coordinated. So the potential is there for more of the same to happen again," said Sleigh. "I'm just overwhelmed by the evil force that exists in the world."

Sleigh's story is just one of the thousands that could be told about the many escapes from the towers and the buildings around them. Sleigh is unique in that he may have been the last one out from so high up, but he is not unique in that many others had similar experiences. That is why his story is told here, because he helps us to see what it was like for so very many.

CHAPTER 2

Unity From Ground Zero

The earliest reports of the first crash – American Airlines Flight 11 hitting the north tower of the World Trade Center – were filled with confusion, and with more questions than answers. Was this an accident? On a cloudy 1945 May morning at about 10 A.M., a B-25 bomber had smashed into the 79th Floor of the Empire State Building, killing 14 people. In 1946 another military plane, lost in fog, ran into the 58th Floor of a building on Wall Street. Only the five men in its flight crew died.

But on this sunny morning – September 11, 2001 – just 15 minutes after the first crash, United Airlines Flight 175 slammed dead-center through one side of the south tower and exploded in flames. It was clear that America was under attack.

The first reports of thousands of human deaths came when the south tower collapsed, killing hundreds of police, firemen, rescue workers, and uncounted thousands of office workers inside. Police and firemen form a bond with each other, a brotherhood of civilization's protectors that knows no geographic boundaries. Word of the loss of so many brothers tugged at the hearts of police and firefighters, active and retired, all over the country.

Throughout the area surrounding Manhattan, police officers, firemen, emergency medical technicians, construction workers, search and rescue specialists, and others dropped what they were doing and headed to New York any way they could. They knew they had talents or equipment that would be useful in the search for survivors.

". . . he saw people jump from the towers to their deaths . . . One . . . landed right on a fireman and killed him instantly."

The call went out to many police and fire departments in Connecticut, New York State, New Jersey, and Pennsylvania for volunteers who could deploy to help in Manhattan. Retired police and firefighters were also asked to join the effort.

This is the story of just one of the hundreds who rushed to the aid of their fallen brothers – one man who is typical of the many heroes who wanted to help save a life, or just provide some strength at a time of need.

Bill Bresnahan is not special or unique. He does not want to be called a hero. His story is worth telling because it is so typical of what many other rescue workers experienced. His story helps us appreciate all the rescue workers.

Bresnahan was one of the most highly decorated members of the Philadelphia Police Department. As a member of its SWAT team he was nearly killed by bad guys, suffering injuries that forced his early retirement.

He now provides executive protection services and was doing that job when the news came over the radio about the tragedy in New York City. He knew that Philadelphia police and firemen would be needed urgently in New York, and Bresnahan knew that he had to help. His client agreed to let him go, so he quickly packed his SWAT team gear and headed up the turnpike to Manhattan.

The turnpike was virtually empty. Only emergency vehicles were allowed through. Bresnahan carries special identification and police "dog tags" that enable him to help in such circumstances, so he was able to enter the turnpike.

"I was the only personal automobile on this roadway," Bresnahan explained. "Police cars, fire engines, EMTs were passing me like I was standing still. I was doing 95 to 100 all the way, but I couldn't keep up with them. When I reached a point where I needed to get off, I couldn't. Salt trucks had been parked to seal off the ramp, and nobody was in them to move them. So I kept going."

At each exit he found more unmanned salt trucks blocking the way, so he kept speeding north, not knowing how he would get to Manhattan. Bresnahan, a faithful Christian, says he felt a special spiritual prompting to get to Manhattan fast. He prayed for a way he could get where he needed to go.

"I was praying all the way up and listening to reports on the radio," Bresnahan said. "I was praying, 'God use me in the right position where I can be an instrument for you and the people of the city and our government. Allow me to be a benefit and not a burden or a liability.' And I didn't pray for my personal safety. I don't know why. That would be a normal thing to do, but I never prayed for that. I should have, but it never crossed my mind."

"The building came down like it was done by demolition . . . It sounded like somebody walking on crackers."

Finally he arrived at the George Washington Bridge and said a silent prayer that he would be able to get across. The last thing he needed now was to encounter a problem from a well-meaning toll-booth attendant. Never before had he seen an empty GW Bridge, so he was worried he might be unable to cross. It looked as if they were letting nobody through.

"When I hit the bridge I said to the guy at the toll, 'I'm a retired SWAT team cop. I'm here to help. They deployed me here. Where should I go?'

"I showed him my dog tags, and he said, 'Right on the other side of the bridge there's a command center set up.'

"I went there, knocked on the door, introduced myself and said, 'I'm here from Philadelphia to help you guys.'

"'How many you got?' he said.

"'Just me in my car,' I told him. 'I'm certain others are already here or on the way separately.'

"'Just you?'

"'Yeah, and I'm retired.'

"'Pal, we'll take ya. I'll have a car run you right in, but you'll have to walk six blocks.'

"'Not a problem,' I said. And they took me up to six blocks away from that thing and I walked in the rest of the way," Bresnahan explained.

In those first few hours after the attack, when all the New York police and firemen were shaken by the loss of so many of their own, they were thrilled with all the volunteer police and firemen coming from surrounding areas to help. During those first few hours volunteers were needed and welcomed with open arms, but within a day many were turned away.

More than men showed up to help. A lot of specialized equipment and K-9 units arrived with them. One New Jersey fire department donated an entire fire truck when it learned that so many fire engines had been destroyed by the collapsing south tower.

Bresnahan left his own vehicle in the Fort Lee command center parking lot and was driven by the Port Authority to the World Trade Center complex. He brought his own backpack with the gear he would need. The police car could not get closer than six blocks away because of all the debris.

"I walked straight into Ground Zero, right into where the firemen were. I just walked right up to them and asked what I could do to help.

"I had my SWAT team shirt on and my SWAT team hat on, and I had my dog tags around my neck so they could see that I was a SWAT team member. They could easily see who I was and quickly accepted me as one of their own.

"When they moved, I moved with them. When they gave me orders, I followed them. Sometimes I offered suggestions and was never questioned. We treated each other with respect," said Bresnahan.

A Hike into Hell

The walk through the debris into Ground Zero was horrific and shocking in every sense, like a hike into Hell. The trek was short but hard, particularly as he got to the last few blocks. Smoke and dust in the air made it difficult to see or breathe, and the debris made walking rough. But the most difficult part was the sight of body parts lying everyplace he looked.

As the buildings came down, falling debris literally chopped to pieces the unfortunate people trapped inside. Very little remained to be recovered, and the chances of finding survivors looked small.

Police, fire, and rescue vehicles were burned, crushed, and hard to recognize because they were covered by a shroud of gray dust from pulverized concrete and asbestos. Many of the vehicles had bodies in them – or under them. Bresnahan, trained to assess violence at a glance, could see from the moment he reached Ground Zero that the death toll would be high.

"You could smell death already. Blood was running like water in some locations. Blood all over the place. Human body parts, large and small, were everywhere. It was an awful scene like nothing you could ever imagine. There were a few arms and legs, but mostly the body parts were smaller than that . . . just chunks or scraps of flesh. And because of all the dust it was something you didn't realize at first glance," said Bresnahan of the grisly scene.

The walk into Ground Zero gave him time to prepare his mind and heart for the massive destruction, the shattered bodies and property, that he would have to deal with in order to work and help. He said a little prayer quietly to himself, took his Bible out of his backpack, and held it firmly.

Bresnahan looked around for someone in authority to report to, but no one was overseeing the operation. Officials were taking charge of their own groups, so he joined one group of rescue workers digging and searching through debris. Many of the first police and fire department leaders to arrive on the scene were now dead or missing. Many left behind were in shock. Some were digging and searching. Others wandered aimlessly through the devastation with eyes that looked dazed or glazed, as if waiting for sunrise to wake them from a nightmare.

"We just worked randomly in an unorganized way. We didn't know what to do, that was the thing. No organization, no thoughts other than that we strived and lived for finding people in need. So you're just going where your heart's telling you to go. You know, none of us had a clue," said Bresnahan of the work that took place in those first hours after the two towers collapsed. "A lot of us felt stunned, and it took time to work together to change chaos into an organized rescue effort."

He reached Ground Zero shortly after the north tower came down and long before building 7, the American Express Building, collapsed late that afternoon. Those first few hours were the hardest for rescue workers. They desperately wanted to help find survivors, but they also had to set up a command center and organize the search efforts. Amid confusion and chaos when Bresnahan arrived, the emergency workers did their best.

"One fireman sitting on a step was holding a leg – all that remained of another fireman. From the knee down to the boot."

The rescuers knew they were racing against time. In any type of building collapse (typically from earthquakes), 90 percent of survivors are found during the first 24 hours. Beneath the smoldering rubble of the World Trade Center, victims could be bleeding, dehydrating, asphyxiating from gases, or slowly cooking to death. Each passing minute could mean life or death.

When he first arrived on the scene Bresnahan was concerned about all the falling debris, especially glass. He had no helmet but spotted one on the ground. As he bent to pick it up, he noticed a body part right next to it. The ash-gray dust on everything was almost a blessing, he said, because it helped camouflage the carnage.

But some bodies were all too easy to see and very disturbing to the rescue workers. There were bodies in crushed and burned vehicles, as well as under vehicles. A few were hanging high in the air from pieces of steel girders. Others were just out in the open. A firefighter told Bresnahan that he saw people jump from the towers to their deaths landing only a few feet away from him. One such jumper reportedly landed right on a firefighter and killed him instantly.

"Bodies lay trapped under the EMT vehicles, caught in doorways, and even sitting on park benches. We found dead people sitting with debris piled up on them. The bench legs were broken, but you could tell they were sitting on them.

"One body lay burning on the ground next to a burned-out car. The body was already burned and charred, but again it caught fire. Tons of papers from office files covered the ground, up to the wheel wells of cars in some places. Things kept catching fire for no apparent reason.

"Some bodies lay in fetal positions. One lady had jumped and landed on a steel girder, and every time we looked up we could see her body up there. It was awful. We said, 'Can somebody get her down!' Later, that building fell, and I guess she came back to earth with it. She wasn't there after building 7 came down."

Bresnahan, like virtually all rescue workers, said he worked hard to put his shock and grief aside so he could help others deal with their own grief. He struggled to work in the search effort without being distracted by the horror all around him.

Bresnahan knew he could never run fast enough to escape the wall of debris coming at him.

A Catholic priest introduced himself to Bresnahan as Father Mychal Judge. The men spoke for only a very few minutes. Father Judge asked him to help by comforting a separate group of rescuers. Bresnahan felt somewhat inadequate.

"He was a real chaplain, and I was only a well-meaning Christian totin' a Bible. It seemed like the biggest need was prayer, because all the firemen were in shock when finding, you know, pieces of bodies. Spiritual direction was the most important part of that whole 24 hours, other than trying, of course, to find the victims," Bresnahan explained.

"He (Father Judge) said, 'Look, we need to split up. There's just us here.'

"I told him, 'I'm not qualified. I'm just a follower, a Christian.'

"He said, 'Then that's all you need to know. These guys need encouragement and prayer. You can do that. So, we gotta split up, and take your own niche.'

"That's what we did. Father Judge went with the firemen. I went in my direction with the iron and steel workers and some firemen," said Bresnahan.

He said he thinks Judge and some firemen went into a portion of what was left of one of the towers. A catwalk connected that and another building, and a short time later it all came down.

"The catwalk was about 10 to 20 floors up. That came crashing down, which took the inside of the buildings down. I think that's what killed Father Judge and the firemen. I think they were somewhere in or around there. I'm not sure because I actually didn't learn of his death for a few days.

"I learned about it when I was listening to the news. They said they were burying somebody and I wondered how they could be burying someone so soon. Then I heard them mention his name and I was shocked. I couldn't believe it," said Bresnahan.

He confirmed reports that firemen and police received the last rites from Father Judge before they went into some dangerous areas, attempting to locate survivors. Other rescue workers went into the same area and never came out. They also worried that pockets of gas were ready to explode, and that some remnants of the buildings were unstable.

"We were praying with them and blessing them," said Bresnahan.

"Before the second half of the second tower collapsed, I was pairing up with teams of firemen. A fire chief asked me, 'Where do you think you're going?'

"I showed him my dog tags and said, 'I'm here to help. I'm a retired SWAT team volunteer from Philadelphia ready to help your brothers who are suffering here. I'm qualified. I'm spiritually grounded, and I want to help.'

"He said, 'Okay, let's go. But I want you to follow my men and do what you're told.'

"And that was the first team I was with. And then I got taken in a different direction, which was very easy if you know anything of the first 24 hours of anything like that," said Bresnahan.

Because he was holding a Bible he attracted the attention of a fire department chaplain.

"One of the chaplains for the fire department was there from the first call. He watched as all these guys got killed. He was battered. He was shipwrecked. He said, 'I don't know what to tell you. You're in for a rough day.'

"And so we read from the Bible together, and we prayed together and we both cried and hugged each other. It was like that the whole time you were there.

"I don't remember when I cried so much. I don't know if my eyes are burning from the smoke and debris or from crying too much and rubbing them," said Bresnahan, choking back tears. "I cried and cried and cried."

"You could smell death already . . . Blood all over the place. And body parts, large and small, were everywhere."

Bresnahan was again called on to help dig for survivors, so he put the Bible away and pitched in.

"I just joined in and started digging. We dug and worked until we were wringing wet. We couldn't breathe. We lost our hats. We lost our gloves after a while. The gloves got so heavy with the wet and sweat. Nobody used any of the safety equipment after a while because it was too cumbersome and we no longer cared about our own lives. We just wanted to save lives. We lived . . . everyone there lived . . . to find one live body. One live person among the dust and debris that we could bring out alive, but all we found were body parts," said Bresnahan, his voice choked with emotion as he described the challenge and frustration all rescuers faced.

Conditions were so bad that to work for more than a short period of time was impossible for even the strongest men. Bresnahan is disabled, with two artificial knees and other problems from injuries that nearly killed him in his days as a SWAT team member.

During a break to wash out his eyes and mouth from all the dust, Bresnahan looked around and noticed medical people doing little, apparently for lack of directions. He decided to take the bull by the horns and turn chaos into organized chaos. Several doctors arrived by foot from the nearby St. Vincent's Hospital dressed in their scrubs. .

"What do you need me to do for you?" Bresnahan asked the doctors.

"We need a building and tables set up," they told him.

Seizing the initiative, Bresnahan helped the rescue workers and doctors set up a badly needed first aid center and morgue. Police and firemen followed his suggestions without question, and they quickly found a building where doctors could treat injured victims before sending them to the hospital. As soon as the location was set up, injured police and firemen began to be treated.

Rescue workers used this first aid station to wash smoke and dust from their eyes and noses. Acting as nurse, Bresnahan used bottled water and saline solution to help police and firemen wash out their eyes. Workers began coming to the makeshift center to rest and prepare to go back out for more work. Bresnahan soon joined a group going back out to dig.

"We worked Ground Zero in waves," Bresnahan explained. "It was very unstable, and we knew that other buildings might come down, so we were told, 'When you hear the three air horn signals that means to get out of there fast.'

"I asked, 'Okay, get out of where? How do we know what direction is away from danger?'

"'Only God can tell you that,' I was told. 'We can just give you the signal. The rest is up to you, and may the Lord be with you.'

"So we all prayed. They saw that I had a Bible with me. They asked if I was a chaplain and I said, 'No, I'm just an ordinary Joe who believes in Jesus.'

"'Would you like to be our chaplain today?' they asked.

"'I'd be honored.'

"'Because there ain't nobody here who has a Bible,' they said.

"I had my Bible, and we prayed before we went to work. We took turns. I prayed, and then each man said a few words. It was remarkable."

The men seemed to come back to life after praying together. It lifted their spirits and renewed the strength they all needed, said Bresnahan. They were able to overcome grief and hopelessness, and returned to searching for survivors.

. . . they discovered the body . . . crushed in the driver's seat. They were unable to remove the body or turn off the eerie flashing lights.

The rescuers felt frustrated because they were unable to sustain a long-term effort. The air was so thick with smoke and dust, forcing all to retreat every few minutes to restore their breathing. They tried to send others to the place they had been working, but this rarely happened because few could really find the right spot to pick up where another man left off.

"During these breaks to recuperate at our base, we would just rest. Take our shoes off. Let them dry. Empty the water out of our boots. Do something to get our minds off the horror. Our eyes were cleaned out with saline about every 15 minutes. And we would direct new workers, sharing what we had seen and were trying to do. They would try to pick up where they felt we left off," explained Bresnahan.

Time and time again the rescuers would start working on the pile and then would be called back because of safety concerns. Fires broke out spontaneously, debris continued to fall from damaged buildings still standing, and we could smell gas leaking.

"Sometimes we would hear a pop from the pile of debris. It was like a cork out of a bottle but amplified a thousand times. It sounded so subtle, but also sharp and explicitly clear. Well, these pops were explosions. Each was a gas pocket igniting.

"When they realized fires were starting to break out, those in charge started pulling everybody back again. Whatever progress we had made at such points was lost. The piles might shift or cave in where we were digging. Sometimes we were unable to find our way back to the place where we had opened a hole.

"No sooner did you dig a few feet than you were ordered to leave for safety, and new debris would cover everything you had done. It was frustrating and demoralizing.

"The streets were still littered with wreckage. Heavy equipment could not be driven in. The EMTs didn't have any clean area to set up for treating people. But there were no men to spare," said Bresnahan.

Bresnahan noticed one firefighter taking a break from the rescue effort. He was sitting on some debris eating an orange when he stopped, dropped it on the ground, and began to cry.

"He just broke down and cried like a baby," said Bresnahan. "You just wanted to go over and hug him, and I did. I went over and I said, 'Look, I'm not a pastor, a chaplain or anything. I just believe in God. Would you mind if I pray with you?

"He said, 'No, can I pray too?'

"'Absolutely,' I answered. So I prayed and he prayed. He then told me he had a family member who was in one of the towers.'"

Bresnahan was astonished when he caught a man picking up a wallet from the debris. When he asked him what was going on the man made excuses.

"You're not supposed to be picking this up," Bresnahan told the man.

"Who are you? What are you doing here?"

The man was unable to provide any identification, so Bresnahan took the wallet, turned him in to the local police, and then returned to keep searching for survivors. A little later he saw what appeared to be Port Authority police taking the man away in handcuffs.

"Stealing from the dead. You can't get any lower than that," said Bresnahan.

Scattered throughout the debris were purses, wallets, cash, and other valuables. The rescue workers left everything untouched because a wallet or purse might indicate that someone was below in the debris or help to identify victims found nearby.

"The heat must have been tremendous. The body disintegrated when we touched it."

Building 7 had been burning throughout the day. Bresnahan was with a group of firefighters standing about 50 yards from building 7 discussing their concerns about how stable it was. They watched smoke and fire continuing to come from the building.

"A fire chief said he thought that building should be coming down any moment now. He said it should have collapsed hours ago.

"He said, 'It has suffered tremendous heat. It should be dropping any minute. So I don't recommend going near.'

"The words no sooner left his mouth, so help me, than building 7 came down like it was done by demolition. It just dropped straight down. It sounded like somebody walking on crackers. Honest to goodness," described Bresnahan. "We were all looking at each other trying to figure out what that strange noise was. We didn't know. I mean, it was a weird sound. It wasn't loud. It was like a bunch of crackers being crushed and walked on.

"But the next thing I know smoke came out both sides of the building like a fireball. More like a big mushroom. And we all started running. Everyone started running because we saw glass start flying, and bricks."

All the firefighters ran away as fast as they could, but Bresnahan knew he could never run fast enough to escape the wall of debris coming at him. His disabilities kept him off the SWAT team for good reason, and they put him in grave danger now.

Fast thinking saved him. He crouched in a doorway with another rescue worker just as an explosive blastwave of debris began flying past.

"I crouched down in the doorway and, sure enough, glass, brick, steel – you name it – was flying. And it came down. The whole building came down," said Bresnahan of the near-death experience. Many years of training for danger saved his life.

"You don't realize how much you acquire when you go through hours, months, and years of police training until a moment of crisis comes. I've gone through hostage negotiations, bomb disposal, disarming people, you name it. I've been through everything, but I've never been through training for this situation. But things came to me when I wasn't even thinking about it, and I just knew what to do. It had become a reflex, an instinct, almost a sixth sense. It was awesome," he said.

Bresnahan and the rescue worker sheltered in the doorway for almost 10 minutes before the debris stopped flying and the heavy dust and smoke cleared. When it was over, wreckage from the collapsed building lay three feet deep beside their legs. They had to climb half an average man's height to get out of the doorway.

"If we had all stayed where we'd been looking at this building and wondering 'what's that noise?' we would have been knocked down and buried alive. And when the chief said, 'The building's coming down, split,' we all ran. Firemen who left their tanks, hats, and coats later returned to find their equipment buried in rubble. This had been where everyone waited in a staging area, waited to get directions about how, when, and where we went in. Now this spot, too, lay covered with fresh devastation."

Bresnahan spent much of his time praying while he was waiting in the doorway for the debris and smoke to subside. He says he felt no fear.

" . . . the floor gave out from under us. That's all I remember."

"I stood there just praying," he remembered. "I just prayed to the Lord. I prayed for all those firemen running. I just felt a sense of protection where I was. But as I saw the debris and the glass fly past me it was like a typhoon. It was like a wind tunnel, like a vacuum cleaner sucking stuff out of the air from the opposite end. It was flying past like 60 miles an hour. Guys were running. I saw one guy get hit in the back of the head with what looked like a ceiling track for acoustic tiles. He had his helmet on and appeared to be unhurt."

Bresnahan does not know if anyone was killed in the collapse. Most of the rescue workers were prepared because it had been expected for a number of hours. The collapse dampened the spirit of many workers because much of what they had cleared while searching for survivors was again buried. After a long day of work it was disheartening.

With each passing hour, the rescuers knew, the prospects for finding survivors were slimmer. It was again a time for prayer and consolation. Bresnahan made the rounds to encourage firemen. Their closest friends and in some cases family members were lost, and efforts to find them alive were being dashed.

When the catwalk fell earlier in the day it crushed the front portion of a blue van. The rear emergency lights kept on flashing brightly in the evening darkness, which was unsettling to the rescue workers. Bresnahan and several others decided to see if they could turn the lights off. When they opened the back doors of the van they discovered the body of the driver crushed in the driver's seat. They were unable to remove his body or turn off the eerie flashing lights.

Up From the Ashes

Later that evening Bresnahan was asked to join a team of firemen who wanted to search the bottom floor of what remained of a building adjacent to where one of the towers had stood. The men learned that a day care center had been there. They wanted to make sure that no teacher or child was trapped there.

Scattered fires had blazed during the day in the building, but those were now extinguished. Even so, entering a fire-ravaged, structurally-damaged building is a dangerous assignment, but the men wanted to be sure everyone got out. They reached the day care center and were happy to find nobody dead or alive. Everyone apparently got out safely. Then, running on adrenaline, they decided to check the second floor. He was with five or six rescue workers, says Bresnahan, unsure of the exact number.

"We roped ourselves together and we went in there and started digging and picking around. Even with flashlights we couldn't see. It was very hard to see. We're feeling rope and we're feeling walls and feeling the filing cabinets, and when you put the light on it you can see someone's eyeglasses there. Or you saw a sweater, and one shoe there. Things like that. We're in there for 20 . . . 25 minutes. I was struggling with exhaustion, and so was the guy in front of me. I didn't know where the three guys in back of me were. I just felt this rope tugging me from all directions.

"I found a women's body. She died clutching some papers for some reason. I took the papers out of her hand to see if there was something to identify her.

"Next thing I know I hear a voice yelling, 'Oh my God. We're going down.' And boom – that quick – the floor gave out from under us. And that's all I remember."

The floor collapsed and they fell through to the floor below.

"Nobody used any of the safety equipment after a while. It was too cumbersome. And we no longer cared about our own lives."

At almost midnight Bresnahan woke up in the first aid center he helped set up. Three others in the building with him were treated at the first aid station and released. Bresnahan was rushed to a hospital by ambulance. He passed out again and has no memory of the trip or his arrival.

One of Bresnahan's replacement knees had popped out and had to be reset. He had a concussion and was on an IV for dehydration. He had a few minor lacerations, bumps, and bruises, but overall he was in pretty good shape. He was more fortunate than thousands of others that day. He had, one might say, fallen on the building. The building had not fallen on him.

The closest hospital to Ground Zero was St. Vincent's, but it was jammed full. Bresnahan was rushed to Lutheran Hospital in the Bronx. He woke up to discover his clothes were gone.

"They ripped and cut my clothes off me, trying to figure out as fast as possible what was wrong with me. I was unconscious, so they had no idea what might be injured. I woke up in the trauma center.

"'I need my clothes,' I told them.

"'You can't leave yet' they said. 'You're under observation. You had a really bad fall.'

"'Look, I need clothes,'" he said, but no one would listen.

For the next two hours the hospital staff put him through an MRI and other tests. He even spent some time with special solution packs on his eyes because they were so irritated by dust and smoke.

"They did a very thorough job. They didn't cut corners because of the disaster," said Bresnahan. But by 5 a.m. he told the hospital staff he wanted to leave.

"You have no clothes," a nurse told him.

"Let me tell you something," Bresnahan recalls saying in a very firm tone, "If I've got to take your doctor's jacket I'm getting out of here. I'm going back to Ground Zero."

His doctor overheard what was going on and tried to talk sense into him, reminding Bresnahan that he had a concussion and needed observation.

"You're a very brave man," said the doctor. "You're to be commended." Bresnahan stopped the doctor before he could say more.

"I don't want to hear that," he told the doctor. "There's people out there, Doc. They need help. There's very little support right now because they can't get through."

The doctor agreed to release him later in the morning, but within half an hour Bresnahan signed himself out. He persuaded an orderly to give him a pair of scrubs that, although two sizes too small, he managed to put on. He added a hospital gown to cover them.

Showing his ID to a policeman, Bresnahan got a ride to the 72nd precinct.

"I talked to a supervisor and he arranged for another policeman to take me back to my car because I had a bag there with a change of clothes. So he took me back to my car at the command center. I changed, and then I got a ride in just like the day before. The police brought me in, and again I walked the same six blocks to Ground Zero."

Bresnahan was tired and in pain from the fall. But he felt a need to go back and resume his efforts. After what now felt like a long hike to get through the six blocks of debris, he went to the first aid station he had helped set up the day before. He rested awhile, drank some water, and ate a few oranges and yogurt.

"The Red Cross was superb. Absolutely superb," Bresnahan said. He also spoke highly of the care he received at the hospital. Before long he felt refreshed and went back to work looking for survivors.

"Stealing from the dead. You can't get any lower than that."

Sometimes he dug, but because of his concussion he tried to be careful. He helped other rescue workers rinse out their eyes, encouraged firemen to take breaks and eat, and helped where he could.

Everywhere he looked was more devastation. Emergency vehicles parked beside the towers were not only crushed by debris but also burned. Shortly after returning to Ground Zero that morning, he was asked to help remove a burned body from a car.

"The heat must have been tremendous. The body disintegrated when we touched it. It was sickening. I got sick," he said of the experience.

Bresnahan began to spot firemen who needed spiritual uplifting and strength. It had been a long, difficult night. Many were now exhausted and found it hard to control their emotions.

"One rescue worker sitting on a step was holding a leg – all that remained of another rescue worker," Bresnahan described. "The foot was still in the boot. I sat beside him and didn't say anything for a while. He was crying and just holding on to this boot. And finally I said, 'How are ya, how ya doin'?'

"'He said, 'How do you say goodbye to a comrade, a friend that you grew up with all your life and you can't find him? This is all I got.'

"'Well, you pray,' I said. 'You pray for his family, and you give him a dignified burial. Do you want me to tag him for you and put his name and information on it?' But he would not give it up. And I started crying."

The fireman had been sitting there holding the leg of his friend for some time. Bresnahan was in the right place at the right time to help such people in need.

"The whole time I was there it was emotional with tears. But I also never emotionally hugged a man as often as I hugged men that night. I mean, it was like I've known these people all my life. They were family. When we hugged and embraced, it was true love. It was the ultimate of Jesus.

"These men were like little children who had lost their very best friends and family members. They were devastated. They needed another person who could share that. Not a tough guy who would say 'Go back to work.'

"Big men. Big steel and girder guys, and construction guys were in tears. Guys were hugging each other. Just before I headed home, they dug out a pair of firemen that I guess embraced for the ultimate disaster. They were right beneath the fall of the building, and they were dug up hugging each other. They were holding each other in full uniform.

"Another guy's walking out of the rubble crying and holding an arm and nothing else with it. Nothing but a bunch of body parts. A lot of body parts. They had put a request in for thousands of body bags, but these hadn't arrived yet.

"The bodies were starting to smell. The air was thick with the scent of death, and it wasn't a good situation out there," he said.

One group of firemen came out of a building seeking help.

"They were carrying their dead fire chief's decapitated body and head. I approached and asked if they would like to pray. They asked if I was a priest and I confessed I was not.

"'Well, that is a Bible, right?' they asked.

"'Yes, it is.'

"'Well, this is our chief,' they said.

"'I'll pray with you.'

"They put the body down, stood at attention, saluted their fallen chief. They then knelt, and we all took turns praying. We prayed for about 15 minutes. They all took turns saying a prayer."

"... a pair of firemen ... were dug up hugging each other ... holding each other in full uniform."

The workers referred to the pile of rubble that once was the World Trade Center as "the pile." That morning, says Bresnahan, about 50 to 60 workers were removing debris from all over the pile. A survivor had been found, and a major effort was underway to extricate him. A doctor was also there, administering some sort of IV while the work went on.

The rescuers had set up a life line so debris could be carefully lifted and then passed along the line. Slowly they were removing debris. One wrong move could send surrounding debris crashing down on the man they were trying to save.

Hours earlier Bresnahan and others were on the pile when excited yelling began.

"We've got a survivor. We've got somebody. We've got communication."

Now Bresnahan was back, praying for success.

"When they found those policemen, tired rescue workers came alive. We came alive like we were given a shot of adrenaline," said Bresnahan.

But "the pile" was very dangerous and unstable.

"There were a lot of pockets in this pile. You could fall right through, just by standing there. The surface was very weak, with false bottoms. Broken ankles, hyper-extended knees, all kinds of things happening there," he explained of risks faced by rescuers.

Suddenly the trapped men were pulled free. An enormous cheer went up among all the workers that could be heard blocks away.

"Everybody was talking and screaming and laughing. I saw the first survivor was crying and thankful to be alive. I sensed that he was thinking 'I want to kiss the ground!' He was just amazed," said Bresnahan. How bad his injuries were was unknown, but this man was standing on his feet.

"As far as I know, they were the last to come out alive. And that was the victory so many workers were longing for," said Bresnahan. "That's when they told us to go home."

"I don't know if my eyes are burning from the smoke and debris or from crying too much . . . I cried and cried and cried . . ."

That experience was emotionally draining, and when told to go home and rest Bresnahan agreed without argument. National Guardsmen were beginning to arrive to relieve those who kept hope, faith, and goodness alight through one of our nation's darkest nights.

"Once I got home again, my wife asked what I thought my purpose was. I felt like chief cook and bottle washer among the rescuers. One moment I was praying like an acting chaplain. At other times I was hugging and crying with them as a brother. I found myself consoling others human beings as if I had known them all my life. Sometimes I was giving directions and orders, and sometimes policing and making sure that nobody stole from the dead. I did whatever was needed, and so did many others."

Bresnahan had an up-close-and-personal view of the devastation caused by a group of terrorists. He witnessed death and destruction at it's very worst as the evil acts of a few have stabbed the hearts of millions. He has seen horrific sights burned into his memory. Even with his strong Christian beliefs, he has trouble dealing with what was done.

"The people who did this are cowards," said Bresnahan a week after the attacks. "Anyone who does this in the name of his God and expects people to believe in that God . . . Well, God is not like that. No god in eternity would want you to take the lives of innocent people. I take offense at them. And by doing this they expect a higher place in heaven? I really take offense at that. For them to commit a shameful act like this, and run and deny it, and hide behind governments, and put innocent people in jeopardy because of their beliefs . . . They are cowards. They are cowards. The lowest grade of human beings on this Earth."

Bresnahan said the government needs to round up every suspected terrorist in America, and even throughout the world, like a drug raid done at three in the morning. "I don't know why we haven't done this.

"Sometimes we're so complacent and wait until they commit a crime, because of Constitutional rights. But as I saw firsthand, and almost every American saw on television, we are no longer talking about criminals who might hurt or kill a few people. We are in a war, and our enemies have slaughtered thousands and thousands of Americans. Should we wait until these terrorists use germs or nerve gas or a nuclear weapon on American cities?" asks Bresnahan. He said a roundup should be part of a world wide investigation to root out all terrorists in every country.

"But the other thing I witnessed is a story of unity," explained

Bresnahan. "Rescue workers came to Ground Zero, and a new unity began there as people from many places came together to work side by side in a unified effort to save lives. The unity spread from there to our entire country, even the world. Good things are coming from this tragedy, and one of those is our tremendous sense of unity."

Bresnahan shared his story here, and asks other rescue workers to tell theirs. These witnesses are the eyes and ears of humankind and can help all of us to see, hear, and feel in a deeper way. The instant television coverage was from a distance and very impersonal. He believes that by helping others know what it was like at Ground Zero during those first 24 hours, our history of the past will be more accurate, and our future will be more caring – and secure.

CHAPTER 3

Have you seen my friend Michael?

"**W**hat kind of world have we brought our son into?" asked patrolman James Fenn. His wife had just given birth to their first child shortly after he returned from working with rescue crews at Ground Zero.

She snuggled their newborn baby as the 36-year-old father sat close beside them. A television in the background flickered with more news about the attacks. A reporter was talking about possible future terrorism.

"You know, we're heading into the unknown here," he told her. What should have been a moment of joy was instead full of anxiety about the future their son will face. Millions of other Americans now also feel this same ominous shadow of foreboding.

Fenn had been at Ground Zero. The misery of the victims and of those searching for survivors was etched in his thoughts and memories. Images of death and destruction kept entering his mind as he looked at his firstborn child.

"I don't think I've prayed as much as I've prayed since that night," said Fenn during an interview from his home in New Jersey. "I mean, I've prayed on the way back home on the boat. I prayed before I went to sleep. I prayed the next day. I think I've prayed every day since this has happened. I think this is just the beginning of something we've just never seen before," said the eight-year veteran Rumson, New Jersey, patrolman.

Torn between his desire to be at Ground Zero helping search for survivors and being at his wife's side when his son was born, his emotions ran from one extreme to another. What Fenn had just been through was enough to make even the strongest men sink deep into grief. But he knew he needed to stay strong for his wife and baby son.

"It was a tough situation. We even got into an argument over it," he said. "You know, here you are arguing with a nine-month-pregnant woman. It's like, 'Don't go back,' but you're in a tug-of-war on the inside because you want to go back. I mean, you feel guilt because you want to go back and help."

". . . it's killing him. I know he feels some responsibility . . . there were some young kids in the Company."

At Ground Zero Fenn felt like other volunteers who responded to the calls for help on September 11, 2001. Every nearby available police officer and firefighter just stopped what they were doing and went.

"When the first plane hit, I was at home. Then the second plane hit and right after that my pager went off. It said, 'Entire recall for our department.' You didn't really get too long to watch it on TV because they deployed everyone from the surrounding states. Well, I know they blasted out the entire city and state of New York and New Jersey. I think some from Danbury, Connecticut, were helicoptered in.

"However you could get there, you got there. You got there. They sent everyone from Jersey from where I was over on ferries. Helicopters came in from Connecticut. You had the Air National Guard there. And it wasn't as if they waited to be called up. They just came.

"You didn't have to say anything to anybody. Everybody knew they were just going to do what they could do," said Fenn.

Fenn and other police officers from Rumson took the ferry into Manhattan, arriving about 1 p.m. Others from Rumson stayed to guard the ferry against possible attack. The ferry system was needed to bring survivors out of Manhattan and ship volunteer rescue workers in.

"They were worried something was going to happen when they ferried some of the wounded and others back to New Jersey. At the dock the chief assigned me to get one particular military officer to the command center. They were afraid to fly him in, so they took him across on the ferry. This seemed the most secure way to get him there," said Fenn.

"Make sure you get him all the way to the command post," Fenn was told as they departed for Ground Zero.

Confronting Chaos

The original command center quickly proved inadequate. While a new one was being established, Fenn and the officer decided to get a full assessment of the situation by visiting Ground Zero.

"We went into the crater as far as we could," Fenn says. "He had been, I guess, in quite a few disasters. But even this veteran paused for a second. He looked at me, because we had talked on the 40-minute ferry ride over. He told me about different things, and when we got there he said, 'Nothing can prepare you for this.' But when he looked at me, I saw that even he was stunned. Then he said, 'All right, we gotta get to work.'"

Fenn had heard news reports during those first few hours after the attack. He knew the towers had collapsed. He knew that many of the first groups of police and firefighters had been killed. But he never imagined a scene as horrific as what now filled his eyes.

"The site is huge, overwhelming, I think, for everybody. When you first got there, oh, the bodies! The body parts! It was just awful.

Requested helicopters never arrived . . . conditions were too dangerous.

"I had tried to be prepared," says Fenn. "I was trying to set myself up psychologically before we got there because I knew there were going to be a lot of bodies. The number was a lot higher than I anticipated.

"I thought more people had gotten out than did. I had no idea that more than 300 firemen were dead. I guess they lost the whole first and second alarm assignment and then some. Deaths were so high because the night tour rode in with the day tour, so both shifts of these companies arrived to help together.

"I saw a torso. You knew it was a woman because you saw the dress. But in the debris I saw just heads, a leg, a lot of severed arms. I saw a leg with a shoe. It was strange that it was still on the leg. Almost like frozen in time. And lots of bodies were up on the roofs of surrounding buildings, they said. I didn't see any, but reports were coming down," said Fenn.

"We didn't know how devastating it actually was. They located one chief's body when we were at Ground Zero. We found another in line with the Office of Emergency Management."

The military officer asked him if any other military liaison was present. He turned out to be the only such person on site. City emergency management officials were busy establishing a new command center and needed a military liaison. They were very close to building 7 of the World Trade Center, which was expected to fall soon.

"The fire department was trying to regroup," Fenn explained. "They were going to move the command center to a school because it had land lines. They were having trouble with cell phones. Some worked. Some didn't. They asked the military guy to help them get humvees. They were calling for personnel transports. They ordered up a whole bunch of helicopters."

It would take time to bring such equipment and National Guard members to Ground Zero, but the wheels were now in motion to make this happen. Requested helicopters never arrived because conditions were too dangerous. The smoke and dust could foul the rotors or engines, and helicopter vibrations would likely cause more debris to fall, potentially killing survivors trapped below.

"... the first thought that crossed my mind was 'Oh my God! Another plane!'"

The men quickly moved off the dangerous street near building 7, which did soon collapse, to what would become the permanent command center to coordinate all activity at Ground Zero.

"I was deployed to a room with what was left of the heads for the city. It turned out to be 'the' command post, not a secondary or satellite one," said Fenn, who was amazed to be so involved in helping set it up.

As soon as radio equipment was operational, the command center was flooded by the sheer number of people trying to talk via radio. The command center was a focal point for communication, and establishing both phone and radio communications with the rescue workers and the outside agencies whose support they needed was a major task.

"There were so many radio transmissions coming in when we were at the command post. And they were overwhelming numbers . . . just staggering," said Fenn.

"The military guy I brought there was on the phone with Gov. (George) Pataki or one of his representatives. Anything the city requested had to go through the governor, and he had to have a formal request. Which he did right away. And that started the ball in motion as to getting the military up and going.

"Then they were looking for a current, more detailed assessment, so we had to go back to Ground Zero. That's when I ran into Bill Bresnahan," said Fenn.

Bresnahan had just helped doctors set up a make-shift first aid center and morgue. When he met Fenn he was watching building 7 because of great concern that it would soon collapse. They spoke only briefly to compare assessments, and then each moved on.

"We ducked into one of the buildings where the first military specialist on chemical agents showed up. The military guys had a small discussion, then went into a building closed off to everybody else," said Fenn.

Fenn said he saw no evidence of power struggles over which agency would be in charge. Everyone worked cooperatively and helped as needed. Other rescue workers reported that same harmony. No turf battles marred team efforts to bring organization out of the chaos that reigns at the start of most disasters.

"Port Authority Police are assigned to certain things down there. They were the first police officers on the scene," said Fenn. "Everyone just went to work. Nobody said, 'You're this,' or 'You're that.' You just go to work. I mean you just start digging. You start on the lines. You start helping guys with stuff. You help them putting stuff on, switching tanks on guys. I mean you just go to work. You dig stuff back. At one point you did crowd control, and at another point you were pulling debris. It was like organized chaos. And everything changed so rapidly."

"I think some of the freedom of movement we've been used to may be restricted."

The years of ongoing training for all police and firefighters paid off, even in the chaos, said Fenn.

"The FDNY, the Fire Department of New York, had their act together totally. The chiefs . . . they were accountable for their men . . . were well-organized, sending shifts to key places. When I was there I saw this one chief O'Brien from the fire department. He was extremely together. He was organizing. He had his subordinates taking sections of men and putting them to work. There was accountability, and everyone was . . . you know . . . it wasn't a free-for-all," said Fenn.

From the moment he set foot on Manhattan, Fenn was on the lookout for his good friend Michael Chauffey, a firefighter for Engine 54 in New York. At first he just kept looking around wherever he went, but then he started asking other firefighters if they had seen his friend. He knew that Chauffey's company would have been one of the first on the scene, and he was very concerned that Chauffey might be one of the missing.

"They were trying to get logistics together as quickly as possible. The highest ranking official from the office of emergency management was getting over the shock of losing so many good friends and people he worked with. But he was thinking clearly and was extremely organized and good at getting the ball going. The mayor's representative was, like, 'Whatever you guys want. Whatever you guys need.' The police department, same thing. Everyone was on the same page. Then I was cut loose so I could go back to Ground Zero and try to find my friend Michael. He worked for 54 Engine in the city, midtown."

Fenn's digital pager went off. It had a message from his mother that gave him a shudder of dread.

"Your brother's up there. See if you can find him," said his mother's message.

Now he had to find two people he cared for deeply – Chauffey and his own brother. He quickly tried to put his own fears aside and went back to work with a prayer in his heart that they would be okay. He joined in with the many others who were removing debris on the main pile at Ground Zero, hoping to find survivors.

"I saw a fireman sitting on the side of Rescue 5 out of Staten Island, and he obviously was upset," said Fenn. "I worked for a fire department before I switched over to the police department. I just looked at him and asked 'How many?'

"He looked up at me. 'I lost them all.'"

"... they were in a race for their lives. They knew they could never run far enough or fast enough, so they searched urgently to find shelter."

When the attack occurred, the night shift, or tour, had not yet gone home. The day shift was just starting. Both the night and day shift responded.

"I guess they lost the whole day tour and the whole night tour. It was right at shift change. Everyone was still there, you know, drinking coffee and whatever when the alarm came in. The city called for a five alarm initially. I guess when the second plane hit they called for another five alarm. Subsequently after that I guess they called for a third five alarm assignment, so companies were coming from all over," Fenn described.

"On the initial alarm you got all five rescue companies, the building collapse unit, the high rise unit. You got all these specialized units right there," said Fenn who was trained as a firefighter and later became a police officer. "Their initial command post was right at the base of the towers. So they were trying to organize when you had both towers going. I guess they were in the process of moving it back but they just didn't move it back in time. That's when the first tower came down. It seems to me they were in the talk stages of moving it back. How far I don't know. That's what it seemed to me."

Suddenly what many had expected all day happened. Building 7 was coming down. It made a strange sound as the collapse began, and at first Fenn did not know what it was.

"I looked up, and the first thought that crossed my mind was 'Oh my God! Another plane!' Two other firemen were right by me. We all turned and grabbed each other by the back of the shirt and ran for our lives. Wherever you could grab, everybody grabbed each other and we all just ran as fast as we could to try to take cover. And the building came down and then the cloud . . . the cloud, you know . . . I mean it just surrounded you," said Fenn.

"I saw a leg with a shoe. It was strange . . . Almost like frozen in time."

They were less than a block from building 7 and knew they were in a race for their lives. They knew they could never run far enough or fast enough, so they searched urgently to find shelter.

"We got behind one of the fire trucks that was there. It was already crushed from when the towers collapsed. Everyone was just taking shelter wherever they could. Some guys ducked in doorways. Some guys ducked behind buildings. It went straight down. If it's going to go down that's the best way," said Fenn.

When the dust and smoke cleared he was able to get up. Fenn was alive and uninjured. The other men around him were also in good shape. The air was thick with an awful combination of pulverized concrete, smoke from the fire, and a smell that made them feel nauseous. Soon a wind blew in and helped clear the air. His first thoughts were to find his friend and his brother.

"When I went in there, I had black on with my tactical stuff. But after the building came down everything turned gray. You couldn't even see the word 'police' on my shirt. I had to get as much of the dust off as I could because you got stopped at certain points if they didn't know who you were. You had to show ID almost everywhere you went."

Fenn was growing more concerned and began approaching firefighters to ask if they had seen Michael Chauffey from 54 Engine. They seemed reluctant to say much and were acting evasive. They knew that 54 Engine had suffered a tremendous tragedy. They did not know about Chauffey, but they had heard that the entire company had been lost when the towers collapsed. Nobody wanted to be the one to tell him.

"When I couldn't find him right away, I started pitching in and dragging stuff out. Then I saw my friend Mike Goshen. He's an iron worker. He came running up behind me with straps for a crane. He saw my P.D. hat from the back with the city of Rumson on it, but he didn't know it was me.

"He said, 'Rumson? What are you doing up here?'

"'Mike?'

"'Jim?'

"I said, 'Yeah.'

"He said, 'What are you doing up here?'

"I said, 'Everybody's up here. Our chief sent everybody up to Manhattan. We all have different assignments, but Mike, everybody's up here.' And he just kind of looked . . . because he actually works as an iron worker in Manhattan. You just have that separation. You just think that state lines don't cross sometimes.

"He said, 'Help me carry some of these straps.'

"So I helped him carry some of the straps as far as he needed them to go.

"'You be safe,' he said.

"He's older than me by a few years. He gives me a look like, 'You be safe. Don't get hurt.' Then he climbed up on the crane. They strapped some stuff and tried to drag it back."

". . . the firefighters from Ladder 5 . . . all died, trapped in a stairwell of one of the buildings."

Although worried, Fenn knew his brother had come from Newark and would not have been at Ground Zero early enough to be caught when the towers collapsed. His greater concern was for Chauffey because Fenn knew his engine company would have been one of the first to arrive. But he had to put those feelings aside and continue helping where he could.

Heavy equipment was badly needed to begin moving debris. Fortunately, a construction site was not far from Ground Zero. Also fortunately, most heavy equipment starts without a key.

"A couple of the firemen took over the construction equipment . . . bulldozers and stuff. They just commandeered them. They commandeered anything they could get their hands on to cut some sort of path to get into there," Fenn explained.

Fires were burning in buildings surrounding Ground Zero. Debris continued to fall, making it dangerous for the rescue workers below. The firefighters were using tower ladders to extinguish fires one by one. They also used the long ladders to prevent more debris from falling.

"They were using ladders to prop up some of the stuff. Some of the iron. So much steel, God, so much steel. We were trying to prop things up to make it safe enough just get in to assess what was deeper in the debris," said Fenn.

Painful and Personal

The tragedy took on something painful and personal that Fenn and many other rescuers had never faced before. They came to rescue civilians, but found themselves struggling to find their lifelong buddies, their best friends, their brothers, their fathers, or their own sons. And in that struggle, many found themselves.

Retired police and firefighters dropped what they were doing and came to help. When they heard on the news that over 300 of their former comrades were trapped in the falling debris, they did not wait to be asked to help. They grabbed what they had and went.

"The guys who work in the city . . . they knew so many people . . . and it turns out that I wound up knowing so many more people than I ever anticipated knowing. Civilians and firefighters," said Fenn of the selfless brotherhood that safeguards civilization.

Darkness was falling. The day had been physically and emotionally draining for all the rescue workers. They needed to rest but couldn't. They needed food and water, but stopping for such things took precious time that for survivors beneath the rubble could be running out. They wanted to keep searching. Everyone seemed to know someone they could not yet account for. They feared the worst.

"I saw my friend Kevin. I saw the look on his face and he asked, 'Where were you?'

"And I told him what I had been doing. I remember I sat on a bench and he sat me down with me and he said, 'Like, you all right?'

"I was like, 'No, Kevin, I've never seen that, all the destruction and bodies.'

"I was worried because I couldn't find my friend Michael, or my brother. I just started to cry. I said, 'Kevin it was so big of a scene. Everything we did, it just didn't seem like we were putting a dent into anything. It's tough, you know? You train for certain things and you think you kinda can just make all situations better.'"

"I saw a fireman . . . he obviously was upset . . . I asked 'How many?' He looked up. 'I lost them all.'"

"I don't think I'm alone in that feeling. I've talked with lots of people who were there that day, and they said the same things. They sent so many firemen from down here (New Jersey) and all the police departments from down here sent so many people. Middletown sent up, God, they sent up so many police officers I know," said Fenn of his frustrations and the frustrations of so many others.

"Everyone I've talked to has come back and, just . . . I mean, you feel that you contributed and you feel that you did the best you could but you just . . . unless you found somebody alive you just almost feel like you failed. And sometimes it's a little difficult to swallow. I mean you want to find them, and then there's a respect issue so you want to turn them over to New York people and, God, how they must feel about this. You know? The responsibility and everything, because they're the ones that want to find survivors the most. It's their people. You know what I mean? You're over there to help, but it's their people. You totally understand that," he explained.

Fenn said that he and other police and firefighters were talking about their feelings with each other, but perhaps not as much as they should.

Those feelings are very difficult to talk about, particularly with people who had not been there in those first few hours. He found it hard to share his feelings even with his wife. Others have told him they faced the same sense of isolation and horror.

"It was a little tough. I couldn't talk to my wife about it. She was nine months pregnant. I didn't know who to talk to. You choke on it for a few days, until other guys start to come back. Now I've talked to other people who've been there. Unless you've actually seen it, I don't think anyone can understand. Everybody's asked me, 'What was it like? What was it like?' I'm like, 'I don't know how to put it into words. It was the most devastation I've ever seen or ever want to see. It was a battle zone.'"

He spoke of the firefighters from Ladder 5 and told how they all died, trapped in a stairwell of one of the buildings. His friend Bobby Davis had recently retired from that very company. These were the men he had worked with, trained, and thought of as brothers.

"They lost eight firemen. Bobby wasn't there. He came into Manhattan. I called him. He told me. From what I understand he was on jury duty. He left jury duty right away, as quickly as he could, and then he shot up to Manhattan. And there are so many stories of other guys who are recently retired. They left whatever they were doing and they went. They rushed up to the city, to help their brothers.

"He's retired, but he said all the retired guys came out of the woodwork, went back to their firehouses, grabbed equipment, and went back to work.

"Bobby's a tough man, and for him to even show any emotion, it was . . . pretty amazing. You can't really talk about it to your wife. You can't really talk about it to most other people. Unless you were there, unless you've been there. You know, he was there in the '93 bombing. He was decorated for some rescues he made in the '93 bombing. He was just . . . he was so torn, you know. They didn't lose any of his guys then or anything. You know, he was like a senior guy in that firehouse.

"It's killing him. I know it's killing him. I know he just feels some responsibility. I know there were some young kids in the company," said Fenn. Many, many of the rescue workers find themselves dealing with similar feelings and emotions.

"You know firemen. We're always giving each other a hard time all the time. We're always getting on each other, you know. You know police departments. You know, the tough survive. It's not really like that right now.

I don't know if it will change back. I'm sure it will eventually. But for right now I guess it's okay for people to just talk about what they've seen, what they're feeling, or whatever," he said very candidly.

. . . police and fire departments have been training for . . . an attack using chemical or biological weapons.

Davis also knew Fenn's missing friend Chauffey. He had run into him at St. Vincent's Hospital not far from ground zero, so he was able to tell Fenn that Chauffey had been injured but would be okay.

"Michael was getting his head sewn up a little bit, and they found each other. Because they knew each other before this. I'm friends with both of them and they met each other at my wedding and so they know each other. Bobby found Michael and told him I was looking for him. Michael told him to tell me that he was okay, but I hadn't seen either of them. He went back to work as long as he could," said Fenn of his friend.

Chauffey was not on duty when the alarm came in. 54 Engine responded, but he was not one of those first men who went out. All of them were killed when the towers collapsed. Fenn said it has been extremely hard on Chauffey and the other firefighters from 54 Engine who are still alive. All over Manhattan other engine companies that lost men and the survivors are struggling with the great loss they now feel.

"Michael is a brave son of a bitch. He got up there as fast as he could. He got there and he commandeered one of the bulldozers. He was clearing rubble. He owns a landscaping business on the side. Man, he would not leave. He's so stubborn. They commandeered these bulldozers and some front end loaders and stuff from a job site nearby. They just commandeered them. You know you don't need a key or anything. They just jumped on and crashed through the fences, got them down there, and started clearing stuff away on their own initiative.

"The first night he was operating the equipment. The next day he just dug. They got down pretty far. He was one of the burrowers who went down into one of the holes, and he split his head open pretty bad on a steel

I-beam. So he ended up in St. Vincent's and got patched up.

"I guess he went to the firehouse to get cleaned up, get something to eat, take a two hour power nap and then he went back to work. God, he was up there. He didn't even get home until Sunday, and he's got two little babies at home. I kept talking to his wife and letting her know that I kept tabs on him.

"I tell you, man, we took the fire department test together in 1987 in New York. He took the fire department job and I took the police department job where I'm at. We worked together in a Long Branch City fire department in late 80s and early 90s.

"He got where he wanted to be. He always wanted to be in Manhattan. Be in an engine company. You know the pride and everything else that you feel. You know, it overwhelms you. His wife was so worried about him. You know, you worry about his little kids. You know, is he going to be all right? You hear about all the rescue workers that are getting hurt.

"The city that we worked for . . . Long Branch . . . they sent up some of the guys that we worked with. A whole bunch of guys came up from Long Branch and they went to work. They were looking for Michael too. I'm sure everybody has some kind of a connection with somebody, or at least a few people, because the numbers are just so large."

". . . we're heading into the unknown here . . . I think this is just the beginning of something we've never seen before."

Did Fenn find his brother?

"We lost my brother for a couple of days because he works for Newark Fire Department, so he was in Manhattan and couldn't get any kind of contact back to us or from us. It was pretty wild. But he's okay. No problems there. I couldn't find him the first day, but we found him the second day. Yea, it was pretty wild."

Does Fenn expect more terrorism in America?

"I pray to God, 'No!' I hope that Osama bin Laden gave us his best shot and it's over. I hope somehow, some way we can prevent this from ever happening again."

Despite his hope, he acknowledged that police and fire departments have been training for some time in anticipation of an attack using chemical or biological weapons. He said there were teams of specialists checking Ground Zero in case any such weapon was on the planes.

Will fighting terrorism impact our freedoms in America?

"I think some of the freedom of movement we've been used to may be restricted. And you know what? If it makes this a safer place, then I don't have any problem with that. I got nothing to hide, so fine with me. I'm sure there's going to be some concerns, and legitimately so. I haven't really sat down to think about all this, but I'm sure it will be addressed at some level," said Fenn.

Despite the destruction and loss of life, Fenn say he sees some good coming from this tragedy.

"Oh yeah. Everywhere you go around here where I live there's neighbors who don't normally talk to each other who are out talking to each other. People are taking that extra step to talk with each other. Where I live . . . I can't speak for everywhere . . . everything I've seen, yeah. People that don't really talk about certain things . . . I mean emotional things . . . I mean police, firemen. Let's face it, we just don't talk about emotions. Some of those conversations have come out where I've never seen it before. Especially where I work."

". . . you feel guilt because you want to go back and help."

Fenn also said the attack will not cause police or firefighters to quit their jobs.

"I'd say it makes them more determined. I haven't met anybody who said he wants out. I haven't talked to any firemen who said they would leave the job. Most people love the job. I haven't heard of anybody who said they were getting out. Maybe leave and go into the military if that's what it takes, but as far as leaving to get away from danger, no. That's not going to happen," said Fenn with pride and strength in his voice.

CHAPTER 4

The Cry for Help

Our eyes have seen many pictures of the death and destruction at Ground Zero. But the rescue workers, unlike us, also know this horror through their other senses – especially their sense of smell. Many find it difficult to explain that Ground Zero is permeated with an odor so terrible that they constantly feel like vomiting.

Thousands of dead bodies, ripped to pieces by the collapsing buildings, inevitably began to putrify. But these were only one ingredient in a devil's brew. To this human carnage were added the dust of pulverized concrete, smoke from many kinds of fires, leaking natural gas with skunk scent added so our noses can detect it, sewer gases, human waste, and a thousand other ingredients from hell's own recipe.

This stench filled the noses of rescue workers, no matter what masks they used to prevent it. And like a haunting, the terrible odor followed them home in their clothes and equipment

"We were in uniform. And my uniform, even though it's been washed, actually still has that smell. When I smell it my mind immediately takes me back," explained patrolman Timothy Hubbard from the Westtown-East Goshen Regional Police Department, 20 miles west of Philadelphia.

Bill Bresnahan also reported difficulty getting the horrible smell out of his clothing. After several washes his wife gave up and threw his clothes away. Even the washer and dryer needed to be cleaned with bleach several times to eliminate the "smell of death" his wife said they carried.

Hubbard traveled to Ground Zero with patrolman Bob Balchunis and Cpl. William Cahill from his department. They were deployed to Manhattan in response to a call for help received from the New York Port Authority.

The men had been watching the news throughout the day and responded with enthusiasm to pitch in and help when they were asked to drive to Manhattan. They had recently obtained a special thermal imaging camera that could be used to locate people trapped under debris, and they knew it was important for the search for survivors.

"It was just an unbelievable sight to watch all day on television. It was amazing. You know, the incredible destruction and how things happened," explained Cahill. Later he would say the television images did nothing to show how extensive the destruction really was at Ground Zero.

"Throughout the day we just watched TV, and about 5:30 (p.m.) Sergeant Dwayne Minshall, our operations sergeant, approached me and asked if I'd be interested in leading a team from our department. He asked me and gave me two other officers interested in going up. I was just willing to do whatever we could to help out," explained Cahill.

In addition to having the thermal imaging camera, Cahill is a member of the emergency response team, a SWAT team medic, as well as an instructor at the Pennsylvania Police Academy. They departed for New York at 6 p.m.

After a fast, but long drive, they reported to a command center at the Meadowlands in New Jersey. They were told that so many volunteers had responded that no more were needed. Cahill and his men knew they had important equipment that may save some lives, so they would not go home that easily.

"We talked to other people and they suggested that we go to one of the tunnels because the Port Authority had actually put out a request. That's how we wound up in New York City," said Cahill. His determination to find a way to Ground Zero paid off. They reported directly to the Port Authority

Left:
George Sleigh (on right) thinks he may have been the last man to exit the north tower alive, and he is certain no one from above his 91st floor office got out.

Below left: The hospital papers and patient arm band of Bill Bresnahan who was nearly killed while searching inside the remains of the WTC north tower.

Below right: These papers from the debris of the collapse were found in the hand of a dead woman by Bill Bresnahan, and when he awoke in the hospital he found that he still had them.

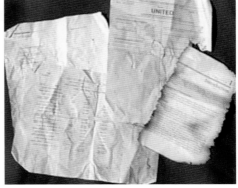

Emergency vehicles and debris from the collapse of the towers of the WTC.

Courtesy Bill Bresnahan

Courtesy Bill Bresnahan

Six blocks away from Ground Zero there is already a significant amount of debris.

Weary firefighters rest in the shade.

Courtesy Bill Bresnahan

Dazed and shell-shocked, these firefighters needed rest after hours of hard work sifting through debris desperately trying to find survivors.

More than six blocks away from Ground Zero a firefighter wanders, struggling with his emotions.

Courtesy Bill Bresnahan

Courtesy Bill Bresnahan

A resting firefighter looks back on Ground Zero after a long morning of desperate rescue efforts.

The initial view of smoke coming from Ground Zero did not reveal the totality of devastation as Bill Bresnahan began his hike into hell.

Courtesy Bill Bresnahan

Courtesy Bill Bresnahan

Steel girders on the pile of debris at Ground Zero.

Courtesy Bill Bresnahan

The dismal scene of destroyed buildings and emergency vehicles where many rescue workers lost their lives fleeing from the collapsing tower.

Courtesy Bill Bresnahan

Ground Zero after the dust and smoke settled.

The NYFD Collapse Unit at Ground Zero after the collapse of the south and north towers.

Courtesy Bill Bresnahan

Courtesy Bill Bresnahan

Construction workers joined in the rescue efforts.

It was not uncommon to find various rescue vehicles abandoned because their crew was missing after the towers collapsed.

Courtesy Bill Bresnahan

Courtesy Bill Bresnahan

The main portion of the north tower collapsed, but a portion remained standing.
These rescue workers watch as the remaining portion came down in a second collapse.

Some of the drivers of these emergency vehicles never returned. The second collapse of the north tower can be seen in the background.

Courtesy Bill Bresnahan

Fire and rescue crews waiting for the "all clear" just on the edge of Ground Zero. During the first hours after the collapse they were often pulled off the pile for safety concerns.

The police and firefighters planned rescue efforts in small groups like this one until a command center was formed to coordinate efforts on a larger scale.

Courtesy Bill Bresnahan

Courtesy Bill Bresnahan

Rescue crews look at the area where hundreds of their comrades were now buried under debris, but it wasn't safe to go in to attempt a rescue.

Lt.Maurice Ottalia, Sgt. Pat O'Flaherty, and Patrolman James Fenn.

Courtesy Bill Bresnahan

Courtesy Bill Bresnahan

Fenn and O'Flaherty discuss the needs of rescue workers and attempt communications to coordinate with other rescuers.

Firefighters were ready to go back to Ground Zero and were organizing search crews.

Courtesy Bill Bresnahan

Courtesy Bill Bresnahan

Fenn, O'Flaherty, and other rescue workers as they were taking a break and planning their next attempt.

Ottalia, O'Flaherty looking towards Ground Zero just after the air cleared enough to assess the situation.

Courtesy Bill Bresnahan

Ottolia trying to coordinate efforts by radio as Fenn and other rescue workers keep an eye on the dangerous situation at Ground Zero in front of them, just prior to the collapse of building 7.

After the loss of many fire engines when the two towers collapsed additional trucks like these had to be brought in.

Courtesy Bill Bresnahan

Courtesy Bill Bresnahan

Bill Bresnahan with a Catholic priest standing by the first aid station he helped to set up. The two helped bring spiritual relief to others.

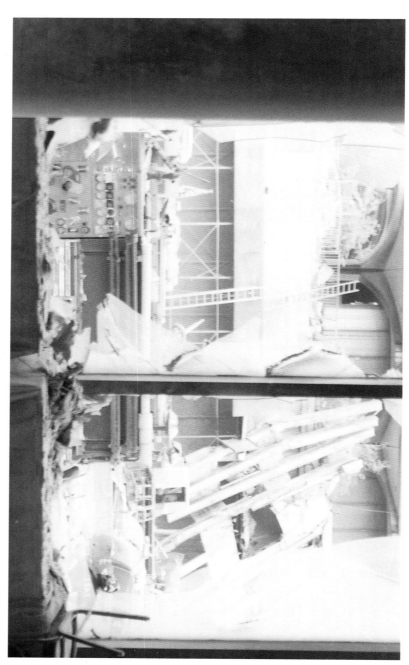

Looking out from the first aid station at the remains of the WTC at Ground Zero.

Courtesy Bill Bresnahan

Courtesy Bill Bresnahan

Bill Bresnahan carried used large bottles of water to help rinse the smoke and dust from the eyes of rescue workers.

Building 3 was selected to serve as a first aid station and temporary morgue.

Courtesy Bill Bresnahan

Building 3 had to be used despite the devastation.

Dust and debris was found blocks from the Ground Zero.

Courtesy Bill Bresnahan

The inside of building 3 was devastated, but structurally sound.

Doctors who volunteered.

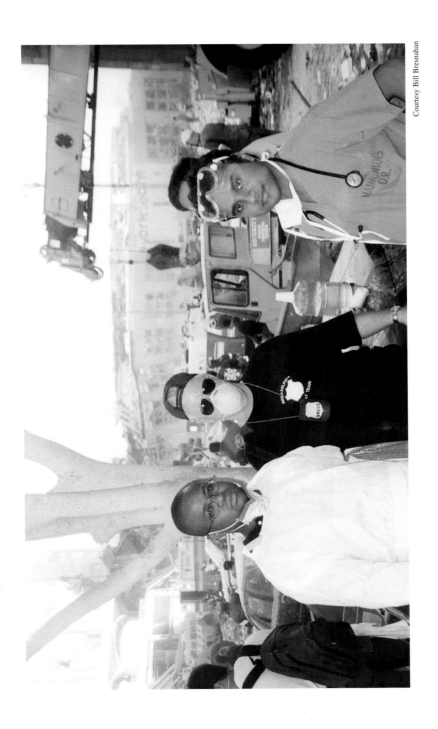

Bill Bresnahan with some of the doctors he helped.

DAVID BRESNAHAN

Building 3 provided the space that was expected to be needed to treat injured survivors and rescue workers.

Courtesy Bill Bresnahan

Courtesy Bill Bresnahan

Later that first night Bill Bresnahan would be brought to this very first aid station he helped set up after he was injured in a building he was helping to search.

Strange "groaning" sounds were coming from building 7, the American Express building. All rescuers were called out away from the area knowing it was ready to come down.

Courtesy Bill Bresnahan

Courtesy Bill Bresnahan

These firefighters and rescue workers are watching for the anticipated collapse of building 7. Just moments after this photo was taken the building did indeed come down.

The raging fire from the American Express building was so intense that no attempt could be made to try to put it out.

Courtesy Bill Bresnahan

The collapse of building 7, the American Express building seen moments after the collapse began.

Rescue workers ran for their lives as this massive wall of debris rushed towards them as building 7 collapsed.

Courtesy Bill Bresnahan

Courtesy Bill Bresnahan

Rescue workers watch as building 7 collapses and the smoke and debris envelope nearby buildings.

It was not safe to return to Ground Zero for some time after the collapse of building 7 because it took time for everything to settle.

Courtesy Bill Bresnahan

Courtesy Bill Bresnahan

Building 7 collapse forced rescue crews to pull back for a time.

The American Express building disintegrates.

Courtesy Bill Bresnahan

Emergency vehicles that responded to the first alarm were completely destroyed when the south tower suddenly came crashing down.

Crushed and burned vehicles.

Courtesy Bill Bresnahan

Courtesy Bill Bresnahan

All buildings surrounding Ground Zero were heavily damaged.

Fires broke out spontaneously throughout Ground Zero and the surrounding area.

Courtesy Bill Bresnahan

Debris and destruction with what is left of one of the towers in the background.

Rescue workers had trouble organizing their efforts prior to the establishment of a command center.

Courtesy Bill Bresnahan

Courtesy Bill Bresnahan

Bill Bresnahan told of a charred body that suddenly ignited in flames again.

Firefighters planning a search of the pile at Ground Zero.

Courtesy Bill Bresnahan

This car contained a body so badly burned that it disintegrated when touched by rescue workers.

Firefighters discussing what to do just after the catwalk behind them collapsed onto the street below.

Courtesy Bill Bresnahan

Courtesy Bill Bresnahan

A small crane was brought in to help remove debris.

The catwalk once connected buildings high above the street.

Courtesy Bill Bresnahan

A crane used in the search and rescue effort.

Courtesy Bill Bresnahan

Firefighters trying to determine if anyone was trapped by the falling catwalk.

Courtesy Bill Bresnahan

Courtesy Bill Bresnahan

Rescue workers searching around the catwalk.

A van was crushed by the catwalk collapse, instantly killing the drive.

Courtesy Bill Bresnahan

Courtesy Bill Bresnahan

The collapsed catwalk with smoke coming from Ground Zero.

Courtesy Bill Bresnahan

All that remained of the north tower was this building that was adjacent to the tower.

The small portion of the north tower containing the children's day care center on the first floor. Bill Bresnahan helped search that area, then was nearly killed as the floor collapsed.

A police car caught in the debris from the tower collapse.

Firefighters planning another search and rescue effort.

Courtesy Bill Bresnahan

The crumpled portion of the top of the building was said to have been caused by a falling portion of the plane that hit the tower. Plane parts were found on the ground below this part of the building.

Courtesy Bill Bresnahan

Construction workers who volunteered to help in the rescue effort.

Courtesy Bill Bresnahan

Construction workers helped with heavy equipement.

Courtesy Bill Bresnahan

Firefighters by a flag that survived the collapse at Ground Zero.

Firefighters searched through rubble to find survivors after a catwalk collapsed.

Courtesy Bill Bresnahan

With destruction all around, the U.S. flag flies on.

The flag flies on.

The damage to buildings adjacent to Ground Zero.

NYFD working on the many fires that continued to burn in the debris piles of Ground Zero.

Courtesy Bill Bresnahan

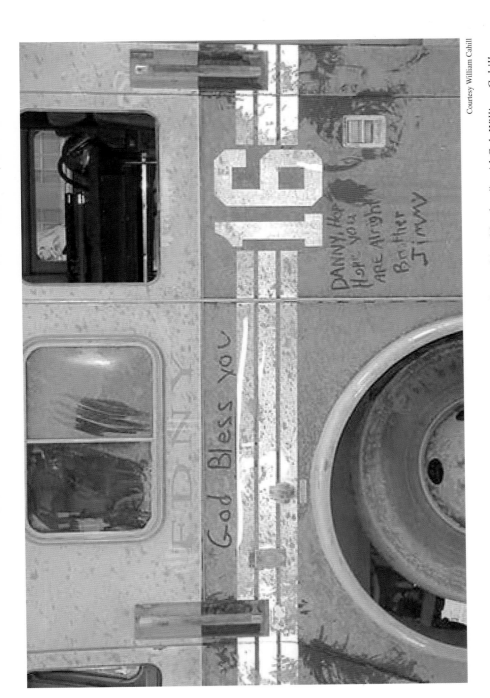

"When I saw the writing on the truck I froze. It was devastating to read something like that," said Cpl. William Cahill.

A portion of the remains of the WTC complex around the corner from Church and Day.

Courtesy William Cahill

Courtesy William Cahill

Rescue workers were not able to breathe very well and had to put on masks, which did little to keep out the terrible smell and thick dust and smoke.

Officer Timothy Hubbard looking on as work continues at Ground Zero.

Courtesy William Cahill

A fire truck that arrived after the collapse sits at the very edge of the main pile at Ground Zero with the remains of a police car to the right.

Courtesy William Cahill

Cpl. William Cahill.

Courtesy William Cahill

Courtesy William Cahill

Officer Timothy Hubbard standing in front of the main pile at Ground Zero.

One of several triage centers surrounding Ground Zero. The National Guard was there to help.

Courtesy William Cahill

A demolished police car. There was a tremendous loss of vehicles. Cpl. Cahill said he and his men searched destroyed vehicles for survivors and for bodies.

DAVID BRESNAHAN

There was a heavy reliance on K-9 units to help in the search for victims.

Courtesy William Cahill

"There was a constant cycle of people waiting to go in and search, or coming out," said Cahill of the way the search operation was conducted.

Police vehicle upside down and crushed by debris.

Courtesy William Cahill

Courtesy William Cahill

"Right in the center there is some type of a monument. That was dust covered and different firemen were writing messages to other firemen. 'Hope you're okay,' and things like that actually written in the dust coating over that marble," said Cpl. Cahill.

Officers Bob Balchunis left, Tim Hubbard right.

Courtesy William Cahill

This crushed ambulance is beside a fire department vehicle that had been crushed and burned.

There was a number of police and fire vehicles that had to be towed to get heavy equipment in to clear debris.

Courtesy William Cahill

Clearing the street to make way for heavy equipment to get through. Many vehicles were damaged and could not be driven, and some no longer had drivers because so many rescue workers were killed.

This police car was overturned and crushed when the towers collapsed.

Courtesy William Cahill

A bulldozer moving some of the many vehicles that had to be cleared.

Some of the heavy damage to buildings surrounding the WTC site.

Courtesy William Cahill

Courtesy William Cahill

When the first fire and rescue crews responded after the initial attack, they parked their vehicles as close to the towers as they could get. This is all that remains of many of them.

A fire truck and other destroyed vehicles very near Ground Zero.

Courtesy William Cahill

Courtesy William Cahill

Officer Bob Balchunis beside destroyed vehicles.

Fire truck at Ground Zero.

Courtesy William Cahill

Police at the Holland Tunnel, and even though they were turning some volunteers away when they learned about the thermal imaging camera they sent the men directly to Ground Zero.

When Cahill and his men arrived they were welcomed with open arms. Travel time and the logistics of finding their way to the right place delayed their arrival at Ground Zero until almost midnight when they were assigned to work directly with a rescue team searching through one of the debris piles.

Cahill's team arrived after nightfall, but even then to see the vast devastation and death at Ground Zero was overwhelming. The men knew it would be bad, but they were shocked by the nightmarish scene.

Firefighters and police officers rushed into a burning building . . . Many . . . received the last rites of the Catholic Church before going in.

"Beyond words," described Hubbard. "It was just massive destruction everywhere you looked. It looked like a war zone. That's what it looked like. It was organized chaos. The massive amount of debris that was there was just overwhelming. As we were walking up you could see the NYPD guys and the fire department guys trying to do everything they could to save anybody who was in there."

Cahill echoed Hubbard, calling the scene at Ground Zero "organized chaos." All the rescue workers used that term but said that it was a natural thing to expect confusion at the start of any major disaster of this magnitude. They were all complimentary when describing how well all agencies worked together as the rescue progressed.

Cahill and his crew granted interviews to help the public gain a better understanding of what it was like behind the police barricades cordoning off Ground Zero.

"The pictures on TV don't even begin to reveal what the real destruction is like," said Hubbard. "The destruction you see when you're actually there . . . there's almost no words to describe it. Just the smell alone! And there were still fires, big and small, springing up out of the debris. And the dust and the smell of the smoke.

"You start thinking about all the thousands of people that were in there . . people you hoped to find alive. You wonder what it must be like for them because at least I could wear a mask to help me breathe better. As soon as that mask came off that smoke got into your throat and lungs and made you choke. It was so severe that you couldn't even imagine what people stuck in there waiting to be rescued might be going through.

"The smell just kind of brings back into my mind the images of huge pieces of building that hadn't fallen down yet. That's a lot of what I visualize. Debris everywhere. Twisted metal. Concrete and everything. There were walls that hadn't completely fallen down and were several stories high. And buildings that still had some stories left to them. It was actually like a lower level of the World Trade Center," said Hubbard.

Despite all the sights, sounds, terrible smell, and the risk of more debris coming down on them, Cahill and his men got ready to put their equipment to work. They had high hopes that they would find some survivors. They tried to focus only on the job at hand so that they could avoid being distractions, remain alert – and maybe find someone under the wreckage still alive.

"Sure, I saw body parts, but I think because it was parts and they weren't anything substantial, or identifiable as a particular person, I think you could kind of disassociate yourself," explained Hubbard. "At that point I was much more focused on the life to be saved than the death all around me."

They went to work on one of the main piles and started to use the thermal imaging camera, expecting it to help them find warm, living bodies they could save. This technology gives humans a new sense, the ability to "see" heat. In nature the Sidewinder and other rattlesnakes uses such a thermal sense to zero in on warm-blooded prey. So does its namesake, the heat-seeking air-to-air Sidewinder missile.

"It's a thermal imaging unit that we recently received from the Federal Government through their counter-drug program. It looks like a camcorder. It's a handheld device similar to infrared. It's a thermal image. It picks up heat sources," explained Cahill.

The men used the camera to scan extensively through the debris. The sophisticated device could see through quite a few feet of debris, so they tried to cover as much area as possible. Soon they realized they had a major problem using the camera.

"For the first hour we used the camera, but it didn't seem that it was really aiding us. We weren't coming up with anything because everything was pretty hot at that point. The debris was extremely hot, so after the first hour we actually locked the camera up. From then on our search was basically just hands and knees. Just digging and moving and handing out pieces of debris. And once in a while we were a human line handing equipment in and bringing debris out," said Cahill.

Although disappointing, the problem was easy to understand. The camera was sensitive to heat, and the debris itself was hot because of all the fire that had been in the towers. The debris was hotter than a trapped person would be. Human body heat, like white camouflage in a field of snow, could not be detected amid debris that was the same temperature – or was hotter.

"Everything was still very hot. I noticed when I was using the viewfinder that I wasn't finding anything. It then just made more sense to move things piece by piece by hand and visually search without the thermal imaging," Cahill explained.

And so they put the camera aside, got down on their hands and knees, and dug through the night and into the next day. It was physically and emotionally demanding, yet they kept going without complaint. The search was challenging. Everyone wanted so much to find survivors, but the more they searched the more death they found. And the more exhausted they became.

"... as he was being passed outward he was ... saying 'Thank you, guys. Thank you so much.'"

"I think you got so caught up in the job you were doing and concerned for the people you were trying to help that weariness didn't set in unless you stopped. You were able to push it aside almost, but once you stopped, once you said we need to take a step back and sit down, as soon as you sat down to rest for a moment everything rushed right over you and you were completely exhausted mentally and physically," explained Hubbard of the tremendous strain they were all experiencing.

Police and firefighters must participate in extensive ongoing training to hone and improve their skills in many areas. Many hundreds of hours are spent improving their ability to deal with every imaginable challenge. Cahill brought his cameras because he participates in such training. He also teaches at the police academy and wanted to use the photos for future training. A number of those photographs were generously donated by Cahill for use in this book.

"I took those photographs during each break primarily to use in training. I'm an instructor at the police academy, and I was hoping to use some of that," said Cahill. Although he said the planning he has had in the past was very helpful to him, it was virtually impossible to be ready for such devastation.

"I'll be honest with you. You can do all the pre-planning in the world, but there's no pre-planning that will prepare you for something like this. Complete devastation. It's unbelievable, even when I think back," he added.

The rescue workers are trained in ways to help people in danger, but they are also trained to avoid injury themselves. They cannot help anyone if they, too, become victims.

"We were all determined to do what we could for the victims. Then, also, we wanted to make sure each of us was okay. We'd see somebody in the line ready collapse, so we'd talk to them and next thing you know they'd take a little break. They needed a break but they were so overworked, so overwhelmed with everything. There were some guys that had just gotten to a point where they were collapsing," Cahill said.

The teamwork and united effort by all agencies was a significant factor in the early rescue efforts.

"I think we were as well prepared as anybody could be, yes. I think because it was such a massive, massive scene. Even so, as big as it was the efforts put forth by everybody there, you just kind of knew where to fit in. Everybody knew what they needed to do. If somebody saw a hole that needed to be filled to do this job or that job, somebody would step up and fill in," said Hubbard.

They all said that everyone worked well together without any struggles for power or authority. No egos, and no turf battles.

"Not in the least," said Hubbard. "Other times, putting this situation aside, you hear of things like that between fire and police and what not, but everybody was just working one right along with the other. If a NYPD guy

said we needed a tank of oxygen over here for the rescue workers, someone would just bring it. It was a very unified effort by everybody."

The long night was filled with frustration and with emotional and physical strain. But morning light brought with it the hope of a new day. As
sunlight filtered through the smoke and dust, Cahill and his men found new
energy and hope with the announcement that a survivor was about to be
pulled from the debris. Rescuers formed a life line, a type of bucket brigade
to pass debris from one man to another to clear a path through the debris to
the policeman found alive buried in the rubble. They had been working the
line all night, and now their efforts were about to pay off.

This stench filled the noses of rescue workers . . . And like a haunting, the terrible odor f ollowed them home . . .

Cahill, Hubbard, and Balchunis felt their tired bodies fully awaken. The
long night's effort was producing at least one example of the success they
and all the other rescuers so desperately needed to boost their morale. All
three men joined the long line of rescuers who carefully helped pass debris
from the area where the rescue was taking place across the pile and out of
the way.

Work had continued all night. Rescuers found the survivor by tapping
on the debris pile and hearing his response. The digging began in earnest.
They soon reached the police officer, but his lower body was badly trapped.
A doctor came in to treat him. Teams of men worked carefully through the
night to free him from dangerous debris that might suddenly collapse and
kill them all.

"He was in there through the night. They would pass in IV bags, and I
know there were doctors going in and out of the line attending to him,
changing IV bags, things like that. This went on for hours. I never saw him
during that time, but from what I understand, he was trapped from at least
his waist down – his lower extremities," explained Hubbard.

This police officer's rescue was the most memorable part of his trip to
Ground Zero, Cahill and Hubbard agreed. The rescue provided a tremen-

dous boost to the rescue workers who had worked so hard, many since the first plane had hit 24 hours before. The amount of debris and precarious way it was tangled around the survivor created a risky challenge for the rescuers to overcome. There was no room for error.

"I wasn't working where the police officer was, but I could see him while he was being dug out," explained Cahill. "He was farther in than where I was located. Their Number One concern was his medical condition. They couldn't see what the bottom half of him looked like, so they didn't know if he had any injuries. Volunteer doctors had actually gone all the way into the hole where he was and were doing what they could. I know they had a hard time getting an IV into him.

"I think it was just overcoming the amount of debris and the way it was just twisted. He was just so stuck in there. Little by little they chipped debris away from him until they could say, 'Okay, it's safe to get him out without injuring him or anyone else."

Cahill and his men were working together, side by side, passing debris as it came from the rescue site. It was a long line that was formed to get the debris out of a very dangerous location.

"He was probably some 200 to 300 yards in from the street in the midst of the debris. To get him out, a human chain formed to pass him out from that debris to the waiting medical team. But the neatest part was that as he was getting passed outward he was looking up at people and saying, "Thank you, guys. Thank you so much," said Hubbard.

The survivor was actually strapped into a basket-type stretcher and had to reach up and take his oxygen mask off in order to talk to them. As he passed in front of Cahill's men, the rescued officer took his mask off and thanked them.

"That will stay with me more than anything else," said Cahill of the experience.

"It's something I'll never forget," commented Hubbard.

There was a loud cheer and lots of applause as the officer came out and was loaded into a waiting ambulance. Groups of workers throughout the area, too far away to even see what was happening, heard the cheers and joined in. They knew that the only thing that could generate this kind of response after a long night was a successful rescue.

Cahill said he believes this was the last, or next to the last, survivor to be found alive. But he and his men never did hear the name of the officer.

They knew only that a brother officer had been trapped and needed help. That's all they needed to know.

The rescuers felt a renewed life and energy. Inspired and uplifted, they went back to work on the several piles of debris seeking more signs of survivors. But the debris was still too hot, and the thermal imaging camera still would not work.

"The pictures on TV don't even begin to reveal what the real destruction is like."

"Everything was just twisted metal everywhere covered with the dust, and then things were hot," explained Cahill. "There were I-beams that were extremely hot. Small fires around us constantly kept re-igniting. Most of the metal we were on was wet. That caused all kinds of hazards. When they brought in heavy equipment, the pile started shifting. That was a pretty scary deal for us.

"They brought in heavy equipment, actually front-end loaders, and moved the debris we were piling up. When they pushed that debris, the ground would move and shake from vibrations. Debris would fall from the buildings that were still standing. It was unbelievable."

The use of the heavy equipment brought concern. The vibrations and pressure it created could cause the piles to shift and collapse further, endangering rescuers and anyone caught in pockets below. For that reason these machines worked only on the outer edges of the debris.

"Yea, at one point on Wednesday morning they started to bring in some heavy equipment to move some debris along the outer edges," said Hubbard. "Every so often you would feel the vibrations, and I don't think it was the vibrations of the buildings getting ready to fall. I think it was vibrations the heavy equipment was sending through the debris. You know, they made you pause for a minute and look back and make sure the buildings around you were still doing what they were supposed to."

The team from Pennsylvania was now exhausted. It was time to leave. Theirs was an experience none wanted ever to repeat, but they also said that some good came of it.

"It was difficult, but until we left it (emotion) really didn't hit me," said Cahill about his personal feelings as he reflected on his experience. "It was such a devastating thing. And to see the grief on the New York City cops and the New York City firemen. The grief on their faces. Their determination gave us determination to continue. It was amazing.

"We were working with cops in an environment we never worked in before. But we were all on the same team and everybody knew what needed to be done. We didn't have to communicate when we were going to grab something, or move something, or attempt to move up on another section of debris. It was unbelievable how the teamwork happened. Everybody was just so focused that we just worked together to find more survivors. That was what we were real determined to do."

At times, even big, tough policemen had to take some time to just let it all out. Fortunately they were able to help one another other deal with those moments, regain strength, and move on.

"I actually experienced that myself," said Cahill. "I actually cried with another guy. It was just unbelievable. And one thing that was nice is that we have a chaplain with our department and he was there to greet us when we got back. That made our return much easier. That was a real positive thing for us when we got back to talk to him."

Hubbard said the only thing he had to give him strength to deal with it all was his faith in God.

"I think the biggest thing that helped me through both the physical and emotional strain was just knowing that, by just taking a minute and even though I'm still working, praying. And asking that I can have that extra effort and that extra strength that I need to get the job done," explained Hubbard.

He said he was not the only one who prayed.

"... I was much more focused on the life to be saved than on the death all around me."

"You'd see firemen and policemen, mostly from the New York City units. Basically they'd just be down – whether they were resting or not I can't say – they'd be down on one knee just kind of having their head bowed and their eyes closed. Certainly it appeared that they could have been taking a moment and just talking with God and asking for His hand to help hold them up.

"I was raised in a Christian home. Ever since I can remember I have always been somebody who . . . you know I went to a Christian high school . . . and it's always been something I've been very focused on in my life. My faith has always been very, very important to me in everything, in all aspects of my life," explained Hubbard.

Both Hubbard and Cahill said they fully expect more terrorist attacks on America, and the challenge for everyone in the country will be great.

In light of his strong Christian faith, what does Hubbard think about the terrorists who did this?

"You begin to think about that, and after a while you almost feel sorry for them. Their life is so focused on something that's so wrong and so inhumane. Their focus is to destroy Christianity and innocent humans. I actually started to feel sorry that they had to live like that. Over the long-term, I think it's going to be a situation for America and the world that no one has been exposed to yet in terms of battling people who feel that way."

The actions of those terrorists brought death and destruction to innocent people. Lives were destroyed, families will be forever damaged, and life in the U.S. will never be the same. Firefighters and police officers rushed into a burning building to save the lives of others. Many asked for and receive the last rites of the Catholic Church before going in.

Did the firefighters and police know that they were putting themselves in grave danger in an effort to save lives?

"Absolutely," said Cahill. "They did it for their country. There's no doubt about it. It's a direct result of what those good people did that they lost their lives. They actually gave their lives for others."

What would you say to their children?

"I would want them to know that their father or mother was an absolute hero of our country," said Cahill. "No doubt about it. Those people went in there knowing the risks. They took those risks to save lives. And as a result they saved many, many lives. They're absolute heroes. They should be remembered forever.

"That whole experience has changed me forever. I'll never forget helping to carry out that officer. I'll never forget all those grieving people. I think it's made me a better person."

CHAPTER 5

Organized Chaos

Pat O'Flaherty grew up on the streets of Dublin, Ireland. Like many an Irish youth he dreamed of seeking his fortune in America. Ireland's greatest export has been it's people, the saying goes, and O'Flaherty became one of its finest.

Americans of Irish descent make up about 40 percent of the police and fire forces in New York City (the traditional Irish professions) according to the *Irish Voice*. A large number of undocumented Irish also work in New York, particularly in the construction trades. Many construction workers were lost from the attacks when the towers fell. News reports estimate that at least 30 who died were undocumented Irish natives.

"The Irish feel a very deep affinity to this because a lot of those police and firefighters were Irish. My heart goes out," said O'Flaherty.

Like so many others, O'Flaherty first learned of the attack on the World Trade Center as he watched the morning news on television. When the immensity of the loss became obvious after the collapse of the towers, he knew he had to do something to help. He is now a sargeant in the New

Jersey National Guard and has served for many years, including a tour of duty during Desert Storm.

"I was wrestling with my conscience because I wasn't on orders," O'Flaherty explained. Even though there was no call-up as yet, he decided to jump into his uniform and see what he could do to help. Sgt. O'Flaherty headed for the ferry with the hope he could get to Manhattan.

"When you see firefighters running like hell and jumping through plate glass windows, you know you've got a problem."

"I frankly am a little concerned that they may try and bust me down in rank. I don't know if they will or not. I felt that I had to get over there, and I felt it was more important that I was in uniform because people respond better in emergencies, and it really did work well," explained O'Flaherty.

First he spent some time helping survivors who were coming out of Manhattan on the C Street Ferry.

"As I saw them coming off shell-shocked, suffering from smoke inhalation, all covered in dust. I was wrestling with my conscience. I knew I needed to help on the other end," said O_Flaherty.

He decided he should do a lot more than help survivors get off the ferry. He wanted to go where he could be of more help, so he joined other police and firefighters getting on the ferry to go over as volunteers.

"We came in by boat to pier 11 on the east side of Manhattan, which is just south of the Seaport Ferry. The smoke was blowing, and it was bad. People were running off the boat with masks on. I had no mask because I'd given mine to someone else earlier on," he explained.

A passenger getting off gave him a mask and said, "You're going to need this."

He arrived in Manhattan, asked how he could help, and was sent directly to Ground Zero with a police escort to get him there quickly.

"It was still chaos when I got there. It was still pretty bad. You know, the ashes were still flying around bad. You could hardly breathe," he described. But shortly after he arrived he and the other rescue workers had to leave.

"The building in front of us was actually groaning, so we moved back," he said.

What he saw was a "thousand times worse" than anything he saw during Desert Storm.

"I was in the desert at the end of Desert Storm. I saw a lot of damage and destruction, but this was worse. The sky was dark. The ash was thick. You were coughing your lungs up with the dust. Everything was covered in two inches of this dust, this asbestos hazardous dust, which we were all breathing in.

"... I remember saying, 'Jeez! I just got here and I'm going to die ... That stinks!'"

"The whole place was gray. Everything was gray and full of paper. It was bizarre. Like the aftermath of a ticker tape parade. If you looked at the papers you saw bonds and checks and personal checks. I picked up a piece of paper to look at. It had World Trade Center Port Authority on there. It was a drawing of one part of one of the buildings they were working on or something," O'Flaherty said.

He was working with several others as they tried to find a way around the groaning building to get to Ground Zero. As they moved carefully around and through the debris fields, they ran into some aircraft parts. The largest identifiable piece they found was a landing wheel, still completely intact.

"Moving forward again, we started to see human remains, body parts and half bodies and the like. Just lumps of muscle, tissue, you know. There was half a body that had been diagonally sliced from across the breast down to the crotch with a piece of a leg. We used cones to cover those up, because we had nothing else to use at that time," he said.

After looking at the confusion, and through discussions with representatives from fire and police units, O'Flaherty realized that he and Mike Moore were the only military representatives there at that time. Moore is a power rescue technician in the New York Air National Guard rescue unit. He, too, showed up on his own initiative.

"There's only 300 of them in the world. They're specialized rescue technicians. They go down and rescue pilots who have been shot down behind enemy lines. In my previous experience I worked 11 years for what they call a Long Range Surveillence Unit. It's a reconnaissance patrol unit. You work in six-man teams. You're all airborne-qualified. You're highly specialized. And you go behind enemy lines to create havoc or create intel," O'Flaherty explained.

Both towers had already fallen by the time O'Flaherty arrived on the scene. His military training and experience had taught him how to look around, evaluate the situation, consider available resources and needed resources, and consider how he could best help the situation. He saw that the rescuers needed organization at Ground Zero. He was grateful he found Moore. The two already knew each other and were ready to go to work.

"I went and got a blessing from the priest, and I took the host. I haven't taken the host in years."

They decided that they should move as close to the center of the destruction as possible. An assessment was needed, and a command center was essential to coordinate the work of different organizations and find resources needed. A command center is a focal point of communication that helps change a haphazard effort into an organized one.

"Now, bear in mind, although we were in uniform, we don't work for the city. It was chaos. Everybody was running around in a daze. We were just trying to help where we saw a need. When we got there, it seemed like the guys who were responding were all in shock," O'Flaherty explained.

"My first urgent task was not looking for survivors myself," he went on. "Plenty of people standing around dazed were ready to do that as soon as they got organized. My objective was to start getting this equipment they needed, and the people they needed, and the infrastructure needed to so that all these rescue workers could start looking for survivors. That was my objective."

Plenty of human resources were available, but no centralized organization was yet directing and coordinating the search effort. Rescue workers had no means to communicate a need for help, coordinate the work of different groups, or request special equipment.

"No infrastructure was in place to start bringing all these assets together. Not just equipment but dogs, people, food, and whatever else it took.

"My friend and I raced up town a couple blocks, and we found a police officer from OEM (Office of Emergency Management) of some sort. I forget his name. What a miracle. He barely got out of the garage in one of the World Trade Center buildings. It was collapsing around him as he got out," he said.

"The dust was so thick that you couldn't tell if it was just dust or was the whole building coming at you."

The OEM officer regarded O'Flaherty and Moore as military liaisons, and they all began to work together. In the first few hours the command center was a mobile bus, but that quickly proved inadequate. They began a search for a nearby building to house the people and equipment needed facilitate communications.

"We found a school where we started setting up. We were the first military guys in that facility to set up a military liaison operations center. All these military people were showing up in uniform on their own, just volunteering. I set up a system whereby we could use them. We used a school that had a theater where we could work," said O'Flaherty.

With the command center up and running, it was now possible to organize work crews and dispatch them to areas with specific assignments. Chaos was becoming organized.

"Then as we started to get organized and get requests for help, I dispatched these guys in teams to go and help, escort, bring food, whatever. We worked together to come up with ideas to get things done more effectively," said O'Flaherty.

The actual transition from chaos to "organized chaos" took place gradually throughout the afternoon and evening. But even with the existence of a physical location for the command center, the biggest difficulty was communication.

"We just started getting a grip on things, and I would run down to the zone myself. I would find these firefighters who do the rescue work. I would physically grab one and say, 'Hey listen. I'm working up here for the liaison with the military. What do you need? What are you lacking? What can I do? What can I get you right now that will get you back to work searching?'

"And they would start passing these requests, and I'd run back up to the command center because we didn't have any communications yet. I passed the word, and Mike started working on the rescue dogs.

"It was chaos for about 6 hours, then it turned to organized chaos. I mean really, it was. It turned to organized chaos when the various agencies started meeting together. They began getting all these different groups to organize, getting the right equipment, and what was necessary to run a good rescue mission."

When O'Flaherty first arrived, he had difficulty getting to Ground Zero because the area around building 7 was closed off. Actual "groaning" sounds came from the building, and it was burning out of control on virtually every floor. Firefighters warned that it would soon come down, but when it did some were still caught by surprise.

"Everything was covered in two inches of this dust, this asbestos-hazardous dust, which we were all breathing in."

"When that building collapsed, about 800 people ran. When you see firefighters running like hell and jumping through plate glass windows, you know you've got a problem," said O'Flaherty. "It was like something out of a movie. The building started to collapse downwards, which was not bad, but then it started coming right towards us. I'm not sure, but I think that building was about 60 stories. So we knew from the destruction of the other buildings that we were in trouble. I started running like a maniac."

The sound of the collapse was like a roaring freight train, growing ever louder as it came closer. The dust and smoke did not just billow up as a fluffy cloud. It had the appearance of a solid wall, and large chunks of debris could be seen flying in and around it. It was ominous and horribly frightening.

"I remember looking behind me one time, and I saw this thing coming towards me, like in a movie, and I remember saying, 'Jeeze! I just got here and I'm going to die. I can't believe this. That stinks!' I actually did say that. But as we got towards the end of the block it stopped. The whole building seemed to be coming at me. The dust was so thick that you couldn't tell if it was just dust or was the whole building coming at you," said O'Flaherty.

He said everyone looked around in amazement at what had happened. Some were overcome by the dust from the collapse and smoke from the fire. A wind came in and helped clear the air. Once the collapse stopped many who ran to safety tried to run back to check the debris for anyone who might have been trapped. Police and others stopped them because it was too dangerous.

"Police were holding them physically back. Then finally they got permission to go back in. They organized and went in to see what they could find," but he was unaware of anyone who needed to be rescued because of this collapse.

The rescue effort continued into the night. Body parts and pieces were collected and sent to a makeshift morgue. It was a grisly task that demoralized the workers.

"They brought these human remnants to the aid station that Bill Bresnahan was helping to get going. Eventually they'll try and identify the body parts through DNA, I guess. What a horrible task," remarked O'Flaherty.

The rescue workers came with the hope and expectation of finding people alive in the rubble. Instead they found pieces of what were once their friends, neighbors, and even family. The anonymous pieces were once mothers, fathers – people just like themselves. A pall of depression and hopelessness crept over the hundreds of rescuers spread throughout Ground Zero as darkness settled in. The work continued, but it was almost impossible to remain hopeful when death hung in the air and lay in pieces on the ground all around them.

". . . we started to see human remains, body parts and half bodies . . . Just lumps of muscle, tissue . . ."

"If they could find just one person, then this would give them some hope again," explained O'Flaherty. A group of rescuers gathered to discuss possible places they might find survivors.

"If we could find a way to get to the underground mall area, we might find someone alive. That guy who escaped the parking garage, well, that's one level below the mall area. So, maybe there's a possibility," he said. Suddenly there was reason for hope, and a group was organized to search for a way into the area to determine if anyone could be found alive.

O'Flaherty continued to meet with rescue workers and figure out ways to organize the search effort so that it could evolve from random, hit-or-miss search efforts to ones that might find someone alive.

The coordination effort was difficult because communications were difficult. Often the easiest and fastest way to convey information was to send human messengers. That task was arduous because of the distances involved and the physical obstacles and dangers in the way.

"There's not just one pile they're working on. There's like six different piles. It's not one little area," explained O'Flaherty. He said television makes it look like one pile in one central area, but in reality there are multiple piles of debris as well as craters. The piles were also very unstable and tended to actually move and shift when workers tried to walk on the rubble.

"Lots of retired and off-duty guys just showed up. No one told them to come, you know. They just knew and they showed up. Like Bill Bresnahan. It was like that," he explained.

O'Flaherty met up with others such as Cpl. William Cahill and his crew from Pennsylvania, who told of his frustration because his thermal imaging camera was ineffective. He also spent time with patrolman James Fenn from New Jersey. Together, they and others ran for their lives as the building came down.

In the morning, when Cahill's group was helping with the rescue of the police officer, a large cheer went up that could be heard for blocks. Others heard the cheers and joined in because it was a welcome sign of success.

"I was a block north of it. You could hear them cheering, though. Oh yeah, you could hear them cheering. You could tell they got him out. It was great. Everyone stopped and joined in the cheers," said O'Flaherty.

Although he has had all types of disaster training, nothing prepared him for the effects of the attack on the World Trade Center. The closest preparation he knew of was a disaster simulation run by Con Edison, the electric company, in which a small light plane accidentally flew into a high-voltage tower.

"The whole place was gray . . . and full of paper. Like the aftermath of a ticker tape parade."

"Who could have thought that not one but two fully fueled commercial aircraft would hit both buildings?" asked O'Flaherty. Now he says that plans must be made for the next attack, which he believes is inevitable.

"I think we have to think of the worst possible situation imaginable and plan around that," he said.

The entire experience has been extremely emotional for him. It has brought him back to church after a long absence.

"I went and got a blessing from the priest, and I took the host. I haven't taken the host in years. It was very emotional for me," O'Flaherty said. He added that the death of Catholic priest Mychal Judge, who died while administering to rescue workers, touched him deeply.

He said there were men who were devastated emotionally by the loss of people they knew, and also by the sights they encountered at Ground Zero.

"They're going to be haunted with these things for life," he added.

For O'Flaherty the greatest heartbreak has come as he has faced grieving family members who came into the area combing through the rubble, desperately searching for a lost loved one. They carried pictures of their family member and pleaded with him, tears streaming down their cheeks, "Please help me." They were just wandering the area, not really knowing what to do. Crushed by their loss.

"It's very heartbreaking. Sometimes I go off by myself for a while to deal with it, you know," said O'Flaherty.

This book covers the first 24 hours after the attack, but it is important to note that O'Flaherty came home only to sleep and continued to work at Ground Zero day after day.

CHAPTER 6

Mass Exodus

"It's coming down! It's coming down! Oh my God, run!"
Screams filled the air outside the south tower of the World Trade Center at 9:55 A.M. the morning of September 11, 2001, less than an hour after United Airlines flight 175 crashed into it.

People who had escaped from the towers, including police, firefighters, and other rescue workers, were running for their lives. Some took shelter inside, beside, or beneath fire and police vehicles that littered the streets around the tower. Most of those vehicles would be crushed by falling debris, and many also caught fire and were incinerated.

Hundreds of rescue workers and thousands of civilians were trapped inside the tower when it came down, and more were buried alive by the debris. As the tower literally disintegrated and collapsed upon itself, massive chunks of concrete and steel rained death on the people in the streets below.

The debris also damaged other buildings. The north tower was badly damaged at its base by falling debris, and fires ignited in its bottom floors from flaming rubble and gas explosions. Building 7, the American Express Building, also suffered structural damage and flames rapidly spread from its top to bottom.

Other buildings throughout the complex were heavily damaged and also began burning. The blazes were too extensive for firefighters to control or extinguish. They turned their efforts to bringing people to safety. They knew the intense heat from the fires would soon soften the beams and bring the north tower and building 7 down as well.

Lt. Maurice Ottolia, 46, of Brooklyn North Narcotics stood at the intersection of West Street and Liberty, unable to believe that what his eyes beheld was real.

"It was like 'Apocalypse Now' and 'Dante's Inferno' and a few other such things all wrapped into one," said Ottolia.

"They looked like zombies. . . . No expression on their faces. Just a blank stare."

That morning Ottolia was getting ready for work and was flipping through the channels on his television when he saw a picture of the World Trade Center with one of the towers burning. He didn't think it was real, but he was curious so he stopped and watched for a moment.

"I'm thinking it's some kind of, you know, video game or they're reviewing some film for special effects," explained Ottolia. Nowadays video games and Hollywood magic have made it almost impossible to separate reality from fantasy.

"And then I realize it's a live news feed. At that point I knew they're going to be mobilizing a lot of police officers and firemen. It hadn't collapsed yet, but as soon as it collapsed I knew for sure that we'd all get mobilized," he said.

He rushed to work, but as a detective he was unsure about whether he would be deployed to the World Trade Center. It wasn't until he arrived and word came of the collapse of tower one that he began to understand how devastating the attack was.

"As soon as I got into work the whole building was mobilized. I happen to work in Brooklyn North Narcotics. Usually we don't get mobilized for things like that. Usually we're kind of on our own. Usually patrol services are the ones who go out first. In this case it was an 'all hands' kind of thing. Everybody had to report down to West Street. As we got down there they started moving people out right away, mostly to the area of the collapse," he said.

It was unlike anything he had ever seen or experienced. Books and papers were lying on the ground and blowing in the air for at least three blocks all around Ground Zero. Dust covered everything. The air will full of thick smoke, and the smell was intense. The north tower was burning intensely, up at the top where the plane hit but now at the bottom too. And other buildings were also burning and damaged by debris.

"I just feel terrible for the firemen and police who were killed. I knew some of them personally. My father-in-law's been a fireman for 32 years. He retired some time ago. So we understand the feeling. It's indescribable really. It's never happened in the history of New York. Nothing this big in the way of firemen and police killed on the job," said Ottolia.

The firefighters and police who survived after the collapse of the south tower wanted to rush in and do what they could to rescue more people. But it was far too dangerous. They had to hold back or they would all be killed.

"At that time the place was still in flames. To say it was indescribable is redundant. The word has been overused, but that's the best word to describe it – indescribable. As you walked up West Street you were seeing books and papers a far as two or three blocks away. At that time number 7 World Trade Center hadn't collapsed yet. That was still standing. They were talking about it and said we can't get too close to that. We can't fight any of the fires.

"It seemed like they couldn't fight the fire in the tower because they couldn't get close enough. We knew it was going to collapse because it was out of control. The bottom floors were gone. The top floors were in flames. The bottom floors were gone because of the debris from the collapse. The lower floors weren't intact. It was right next to number one," described Ottolia.

There was no way in, and for many there was no way out. It was a desperate situation and there was nothing the rescue workers could do but withdraw a safe distance, watch, and wait. They looked in horror as one person after another jumped to their death from the higher floors of the tower. With fire all around them and no way to escape, dozens chose to jump rather than burn. Some were also blown out of the building as explosions threw people and debris to the streets below.

". . . you didn't hear it (falling glass) coming. Sometimes someone shouted a warning, but you didn't know if these guillotines were coming for you, or where to run."

The best that rescue workers could do was evacuate nearby buildings. They rushed into neighboring buildings to warn people to leave before there was another collapse. Very little could be done in the way of rescue attempts until both towers and building 7 were down and the dust and debris had settled. Building 7 came down at 5:20 p.m., so it was evening before crews were able to move into Ground Zero, according to Ottolia.

"We couldn't really attempt any rescue efforts. Some people kept trying to get close on the fringe and do 'search and rescue' in adjoining buildings to see if there was anybody, alive or dead. But as for Ground Zero, nobody was really getting into that area. It wasn't until nightfall that they started moving the debris on West Street to try to get closer. I think the pedestrian walkway bridge number one or north collapsed on top of a fire engine, vans, and ambulances. It was unbelievable," he said.

"An Emergency Services police officer told me they had lost at least 14 or 15 of their own. I said, 'I know we lost some firemen, but we also lost some police officers.'

"'He said, 'Yeah. I was standing here when it came down. I know where they are. I know exactly where they are, but we can't get to them.'

"That's how close they were. He saw it come down. He knew where they were, but they couldn't get to them until the latter part of the week."

Ottolia met up with Bill Bresnahan late in the afternoon. The two were talking with a number of firefighters about the condition of building 7.

"At that point it was basically a waiting game, because when it did collapse I was speaking to Bill. There was an out-of-state police officer with a medic. We were speaking, and even before we had the chance to take any photos, we were all talking about how that was going to come down soon. They were all predicting that it would come down. As we were talking, low and behold, it came down," Ottolia described.

In other areas around Ground Zero rescue workers dodged falling debris and fires, desperately trying to find anyone alive they could save. Their efforts were in vain, and some rescue workers were getting hurt. Many were cut by falling glass and debris. Several rescue workers said they heard stories of firemen who were killed.

"It was silent, you didn't hear it (falling glass) coming. Sometimes someone shouted a warning, but you didn't know if these guillotines were coming for you, or where to run. It was very dangerous," said Bill Bresnahan of the first few hours after the towers came down but before building 7 collapsed.

"It was like 'Apocalypse Now' and 'Dante's Inferno' . . . wrapped into one."

As soon as the rescuers would make some progress moving debris they would be called out of the area for safety concerns. When they would finally have an opportunity to go back they found the work they had done was now covered by new debris and they had to start over again. The real meaningful digging through debris was not able to begin until evening.

"When we finally did begin to dig, within the first hour of when we started looking for survivors, we found two people – just basically bodies. We had no idea what they were. They were just under the debris on West Street there. I think some rescuers found a fire officer not too long after that – killed in the collapse," said Ottolia.

He spoke of the frustrations of the rescue workers who desperately wanted to find survivors. They couldn't get in close enough to search, and when they did get in they were soon called back because of falling debris. When at last they began a full search, in their hearts they knew that the destruction had been so violent that finding survivors was unlikely. Everyone kept hope. No one wanted to admit what they really knew deep inside – that thousands were dead and almost nobody had survived to be rescued.

Other frustrations existed as well. Many police were unable to go directly into Ground Zero and work directly on a pile of debris to help in the search. They were needed on the perimeters of the area to do all the other tasks that fall on the shoulders of police.

"Most of us wanted to be there and help, I mean everybody I know. Every police officer I know wanted to be there and actually help on a pile. Unfortunately that's not what the job requires. You need guys for traffic. You need to secure the perimeter. That was before the National Guard was called out. So a lot of guys were disappointed because they weren't able to be on a pile," explained Ottolia.

All rescue workers told of the horror of finding nothing except body parts or just scraps of human flesh. The scene was more gruesome than any horror movie. But they had to find inner strength to face this ghoulish part of the task.

"I was able to be there and work on the pile," said Ottolia. "When we started pulling out pieces of bodies it was unbelievable. For the past few days I've been over at the landfill. We've been sifting through debris there. You know sometimes you don't find too much, but last night I found a guy's scalp with an ear. That's about all they're finding.

"I know they don't want people to say that. They don't want people to know about it, but that's all they're really finding. Tiny bits and pieces. And a lot of it's being found because of the dogs. They're bringing in the K-9s. They're able to sniff out cadavers. And that's how they're coming up with it. Otherwise it's very difficult, because you're not seeing anything that really resembles a human. And when you come across something it's not very recognizable.

"I found the piece of scalp because I came across some debris, looked, and thought to myself that this could be something. But it was mixed in with a lot of dirt, a lot of other things. Then I picked it up and it started to make some sense. Other people helped to identify that is was a piece of a body. They said, 'Oh yeah. That's what you're looking at.'

"It was a day I probably never will forget," Ottolia said.

Thousands of people escaped the towers and nearby buildings because of the fast work of firefighters, the Port Authority, police, and other rescuers. When they first stepped out of the buildings after the initial attack, they were standing on the Plaza and in the streets just looking up at the spectacle of the burning towers. Only after the south tower collapsed did survivors flee the area.

They looked in horror as one person after another jumped to their death . . .

It began with a mad dash to find safety from the debris crashing down all around them. After the towers collapsed they started to leave the area. The injured began finding their way to hospitals for treatment. Those who escaped without injury just wanted to go home to safety, but getting home was a problem. Transportation systems were all down. Most New Yorkers rely on public transportation, so when buses, taxis, and subway trains stop, the only way to travel is on foot.

Thus the mass exodus began. Thousands upon thousands walked for miles to get out of Manhattan, even if their direction was not the way home. They just wanted to get out. And while thousands were trying to get out, rescue workers were trying to find ways in.

Brooklyn Police Department patrolman Brian Bliss was one of those peace officers assigned somewhere other than Ground Zero. Bliss was helping people who escaped the devastation to find their way out of hell and back to the real world.

"I didn't get to see the terror first hand," Bliss explained. "Most of the people I encountered had been at Ground Zero and were walking out. I saw them on the Brooklyn side a few hours after it happened. They had been walking for four hours. The look on these peoples' faces was absolutely amazing."

They had walked from Manhattan into Brooklyn. The trip was long, and many were in poor physical shape. They became dehydrated, were covered in dust from the debris, and felt shell-shocked. Many were dazed, just walking and walking. For a crowd so large, very little talking was heard.

"They looked like zombies," said Bliss. "No expression on their faces. Just a blank stare. People walked around in awe from the awful events. Now, however, they were walking in an unfamiliar town. They're accustomed to going from the financial district uptown to the trains that carried them home. Now they're walking around Brooklyn, and there's no trains even to get them where they need to go to get home. No trains. No buses. They're just winging it, and not exactly in the best parts of Brooklyn. Not a ghetto, but it's a crime-riddled area. And they're walking around aimlessly.

We were just trying to get them to where they wanted to go as quickly as possible.

"They all had a long, long day they'll never forget, I'm sure," Bliss added.

No one wanted to admit what they really knew deep inside – that thousands were dead and almost nobody had survived to be rescued.

The next morning it was Bliss who met Bill Bresnahan and gave him a ride back to his car so he could get his spare set of SWAT team clothes and return to Ground Zero.

"Bill was in our precinct the following morning. I assume he was in Lutheran Hospital. He was in our precinct in the C.O.'s (commanding officer's) office. We gave him a lift back to his car. We drove him over to Fort Lee. We got to talk to him on the way up and hear about what had been going on at Ground Zero. Amazing guy," said Bliss.

Even though there has been tragic loss of life and destruction of property, Bliss said he has already seen good come from the bad.

"It's too bad it takes a tragedy like this to bring everybody together. At least the whole country's sticking together. And there seems to one general consensus. I was driving past our church the other day and it was jammed. I haven't seen it that crowded except for Christmas Eve mass. On a regular Sunday it would never be this crowded," said Bliss.

Both Ottolia and Bliss commented that they expect more trouble before the war on terrorism is over. They said they expect the U.S. to prevail by rounding up the terrorists all over the world.

"I don't think a prompt military response is the answer," said Ottolia. "You would think being in law enforcement we would think 'Go and get em.' But I don't think that's the answer. I think we need a long campaign. Infiltration. Getting cooperation. Weeding them out. You're making martyrs if you go in there and kill, which we don't want to do. For every guy you kill there's going to be two that take his place. They're going to do it willingly. To them it's an honor to die in a holy war against the United States.

"I'm angry because they have no value for human life. That's apparent because any religious zealots who would go and die for what they believe in like that, they really can't have too much respect for other lives either," he added.

Ottolia, a Brooklyn detective hardened by dealing with the worst of our society, said the terrorists should be rounded up in similar fashion to a raid on suspected drug dealers.

"We have the sophistication and technology, and we can go about it differently," he explained. "Let's weed them out. Let's use operatives. You know we had a really strong CIA network years ago. For some reason our government decided that wasn't necessary. Maybe they didn't want them to be that strong. Maybe we should put them back in action," he suggested.

They knew the intense heat from the fire would soon soften the beams and bring the north tower and building 7 down . . .

Like Rumson Police Department patrolman Jim Fenn, Ottolia said he does not see any indication that police and firefighters will leave their jobs after the exposure they've had to so much devastation. He also said the people of New York City have a new respect and appreciation for the men and women in uniform who protect them.

"The police and firemen of the city have been doing a great job for years and years and years. It takes something like this for people all of a sudden to realize that. Kinda sad," he said.

"I hope the unity that's been formed, the togetherness and the patriotism, that this has awakened in all of us lingers. Job-wise, I hope that the city finally appreciates the job that we've done. That's why it's been a safe city. That's why the firemen have always done their job.

"We've done our job, but it's been overlooked. I'm hoping now that they finally get the idea and say, 'You know what? These guys have been doing this all along, and it just took something like this for us to realize it.'"

Police and firefighters all over America put their lives on the line every day. They sacrifice to do these jobs, because they get paid far less than they should . . . far less than they could earn elsewhere. They work terrible hours. They miss out on important family events and activities. They subject themselves to criticism and abuse. They risk death and painful injury every day, and their spouses live with constant fear of what might happen. These brave men and women are the ones, to paraphrase the poet Rudyard Kipling, who guard us while we sleep.

Let's pray Ottolia is right – that after this wake-up call from hell Americans will reappraise how much we value, respect, and pay the people we depend upon to protect public safety in this time of growing danger.

Men like Bill Bresnahan, William Cahill, Timothy Hubbard, Bob Balchunis, James Fenn, Maurice Ottolia, Brian Bliss, Pat O'Flaherty and the many others just like them are not looking for a pat on the back. But we who see what they do for us should not hesitate to give them one – physically and in their paychecks. We should tell our elected leaders to put a higher priority on the salaries of police and firefighters throughout our nation.

EPILOGUE
By Bill Bresnahan

I struggle as I write this. Emotions wash over me, as the clouds of dust that covered the people and streets of lower Manhattan in the first few moments of a horrible national tragedy.

Grief, the first strong emotion, causes my throat to ache and my eyes to burn as I fight a losing battle with hot scalding tears. Thousands of people dead, and still the count rises. Tears and sadness in 80 nations. Pain knows no boundaries and acknowledges no borders. Gender, age, language, economic status . . . all buried under tons of still smoking debris. The thought of the terror felt by thousands . . . like the man whose last words into a cell phone, while desperately talking to his wife, *"Oh God! The floor is falling out from under us . . . !"* Tears, then an involuntary sob from me – "Oh, God! Have mercy!"

Anger . . . How could they?! As a former police officer, I've known fear. My life has been on the line, but at least I had a chance to alter the outcome. But for the innocent passengers strapped in their seat without hope, thousands murdered at their computer screens, or those making a desperate but futile descent down hundreds of flights of stairs, innocent men, women, and children . . . I can feel my teeth grinding under clenched jaws and balled fists.

As I struggle for control, I lean against an object gleaming dully through the dust and soot . . . a hotdog cart, somehow undamaged. My eye falls on a decal celebrating Islam. Suddenly I am filled with an irrational hatred of all things Islamic. I lose all control and begin to weep uncontrollably. Some of my fellow workers think I am having a nervous breakdown. It is not a nervous breakdown, but it is a breakdown by a carefully cultivated façade of civilized behavior. This is not mere dislike, but an active, pulsating hatred. I must sort this out . . . all Muslims are not responsible. While I can hate the deed, I must not hate people and allow hatred to rule my life. I am not a terrorist, and hatred will not destroy me.

Now a profound sadness fills me as I recall the cries of desperate family members. Names echoing through canyons of New York City, floating over the ruins of the World Trade Center Towers and other buildings which have collapsed. Wives, children, husbands, relatives, and friends hoping against hope.

They will visit the Red Cross hospitals, temporary shelters, and finally, unable to delay any longer, the morgue. For some, tears of joy on finding a loved one with a miraculous story of escape. Most will shed tears of sadness as they find their worst fears realized. Still others must endure the pain of just not knowing. Do they continue to desperately hang on to or abandon all hope?

But now, a strange sensation, an emotion unnamed at its onset. It surges in my chest as a desire to laugh, but brings tears as an urge to weep. I examine the memories that evoke this strange new emotion. Standing shoulder to shoulder with men in the uniform I once wore. Policemen, firemen, emergency workers, fighting as if by instinct, some to their deaths, against the surging stream of desperate humanity. Running not <u>away from</u> but <u>toward</u> the danger. Blinded by the thick, sooty dust, choking, stumbling, falling, getting up, but always moving <u>toward</u> the crisis. Here and there unrecorded acts of great heroism. Men dashing into structures that will soon become their tombs, not pausing to count the cost or consider "what if . . . ."

And now I recognize this emotion. Pride. I am proud, proud of my fellow public servants. The words ring in my mind. *Public Servants* – to protect and to serve, <u>risking</u>, and in some cases, <u>giving</u> their lives for strangers, people they never met and might never see again.

In my mind's eye, I am in the hospital, doctors and nurses working with compassion, skill, and dispatch treat me and others, binding up our wounds, and sending some of us out to make room for others, some who will not walk out.

I hear the stories now of individual heroes, plain ordinary citizens, (can I ever use that phrase again?). The man who stayed beside with his handicapped friend to the end, the men who carried a wheel chair-bound victim down 64 flights of stairs, the man who threw a victim in shock over his shoulder and ran down dozens of flights of stairs, the school teacher who waited till almost all the children were retrieved, then grabbed the remaining children, dashing out before the building collapsed. Yes, it is pride I feel. Despite everything else, I feel this pride surging. I am proud that I was a cop, proud to have been a member of an elite group – <u>Public Servants</u> – but as I look around at the "ordinary" people and their responses to this disaster, I realize I am, most of all, proud to be an American. I'm choking back tears again. I can barely get the words out in a choked whisper . . . "God, Bless America".

I'm drained. Emotions once raw and powerful are now subdued, like a raging river that has rushed down the rapids and over the falls, to rest quietly in a still back water, a tranquil lake. My emotions are still, but my mind is not. Now, not an emotion, but an encounter.

I watch wordlessly as the banner running along the bottom of my TV updates the number of dead or missing. Again, those terribly fascinating slow-motion appearing shots of the towers collapsing. I remember the wounded and dead, some I worked alongside, and, unbidden, a question is suddenly in my mind. "Suppose I had been in those buildings? Would I have been ready?"

Ready? Ready for what? What comes after death? Is there anything?

Some say there is nothing, but suppose they're wrong? Suppose there is?

At this instant, I am face to face with my own mortality. How fragile this life really is. Did I wake up today and say, "This may be my last day on earth"? Did any of the victims have that thought? Does it take a terrorist? . . .

Here's that question again . . . "Would I have been ready?" And now another emotion. One I recognize. I've had it before. It's like an old friend, a comfortable robe and a worn pair of slippers, like being home again. I even know the name. It brings a smile to my face. See, I do know the answer to that "ready" question. And many of the other questions that come. Oh, I don't know all the answers. I don't think anyone does. In fact, as an old cop, I'm suspicious of anyone who claims they do.

Our President, Congress, pastors, people all over the world are praying. Does that mean they all believe in God? Do I believe in God? No, honestly, do I really believe in God? Is God real? Does He have anything to say about what happened, or what comes next?

I'm not a particularly religious man, but I know that I know the answer to the "believe" and "ready" questions, and that's why I recognize this particular emotion. It's called peace – "the peace that passes understanding." It comes with the knowledge that, "Yeah, I'm ready." I got ready some years ago, and life has been really worth living since. Got most of my questions answered, too. Those that aren't either will be, or don't really matter all that much. The questions that do really matter, I can answer. "Would I have been ready?" "Do I believe . . .?" I smile again, lay my head back, inhale and exhale deeply – "Yeah, I'm ready." *

*   If you would like more information about the answer Mr. Bresnahan found, please visit his website www.911terrorinamerica.com and click "answers."

IN MEMORIAM
by Christine Wyrtzen

HONORING THE LOST

> *"You have to do your own growing no matter*
> *how tall your grandfather was."*
> Abraham Lincoln (1809-1865)

America has given us a new generation of heroes to follow. On September 11th, 2001 we stood shoulder to shoulder with those who fought in wars before our time. We defended freedom and country. Our ancestors are proud!

This book is not long enough to honor all who died nor adequate to tell the stories of those who lived. The numbers are too staggering for us to digest. We are awakening to the reality that each number equals a life – a person who was loved and will be missed. Each one has a name, a face, and a family. A three year old named Dana, a Sunday school teacher, a ballet dancer, a fireman, a stockbroker, a tourist enjoying the view of the city from *Windows on the World*, and on and on it goes.

All who were lost died tragically. Many perished instantly at the time of impact. Others lost their lives because they did not have time to find a safe exit route. Still others died because they chose to put themselves in further danger to escort co-workers, friends, and total strangers to safety.

In one of the darkest moments of our country, we began to think like God. All life was precious. All were deemed "worth saving." Lines of prejudice blurred. Economic classes blended. The educated and uneducated worked in harmony. Party lines united with one, strong voice. The mantra of racial biases was mute. All souls – Asian, White, Hispanic, Black, and Middle Eastern – were precious, period.

In the days and hours that followed, rescue workers fought valiantly for any sign of human life, raking through the ashes for any remnant of remains, while those who perpetrated such mass destruction rejoiced in our pain and the macabre scenes. When we cried out, "Look what you've done!" they not only justified their actions but also danced in the streets.

The tears we've cried over the loss of life have been holy tears. Each one that coursed down the face of America reflected and magnified the heart of God. As strangers embraced one another in comfort, we were introduced to a God who weeps. We were reminded that He is moved by pain and angered by evil. Such love can offer the survivors the courage to grieve and the strength to heal.

HEALING THE PAIN

My eyes fail because of tears. My spirit is greatly troubled. My heart is poured out on the earth because of the destruction of my people. Lamentations 2:11

While we live in a world where painful and confusing events occur, they need not cripple us. We have everything we need in God to face our grief and emerge with a teachable and tender spirit. I offer four spiritual skills that will help us begin this journey of healing.

1. **Acknowledge pain.** Unexpressed grief and anger become a poison that hurt us. Driven inward, it cripples us emotionally and can manifest itself later in physical illness. It takes courage to face the extent of our loss and look grief in the eye. God knows the depth of our pain and will never turn away when we cry for help. If we pretend we don't hurt as deeply as we do, we sabotage our own healing.

You, who have shown me many troubles, will revive me again. You will bring me up again from the depths of the earth and turn to comfort me. Psalm 71:20

2. **Embrace tears.** Getting close to God teaches us that weakness is to be owned and embraced. It is not something about which we should be embarrassed. After all, we are not God. Only He is more powerful than this world and the evil in it. Jesus on many occasions wept. He wept tears of grief at the tomb of His friend, Lazarus. He cried over a city because He felt sorry for the people who lived there. King David salted the pages of the Psalms with his tears. No wonder so many of us go there and read David's words. We know that he will express the things we often find difficult to verbalize for ourselves.

My soul thirsts for the living God. My tears have been my food day and night. While they say to me, "Where is your God?" I pour out my soul within me. Psalm 42:2

3. **Develop childlikeness.** Throughout scripture, God refers to His people as children. He invites us into a perpetual, childlike relationship with him regardless of our age. When tragedies occur and we are reminded how powerless we are, we long to know that we have a person to run to for safety. How comforting to know that God gathers His children under His wings, even while the storm rages.

The children of men take refuge in the shadow of Your wings. They drink their fill of the abundance of Your house. You give them a drink from the river of Your delights, for with You is the fountain of life. Psalm 36:8-9

4. **Live cherished.** God is love, yet we often feel that God loves everyone but us. We are dressed in the shame of others' labels, and/or the shame of our sins and failures. God's arms are open wide and He invites us to make Him our home. Not because we deserve it, but because the nature and character of His heart is loving. It takes courage to stretch out our arms and embrace God's gift of love, received in Jesus Christ. How life changing when we do it! We can live with the warmth of His smile on our shoulder and the light of His countenance on our face.

God's unchanging plan has always been to adopt us into His own family by bringing us to Himself through Jesus Christ. This gave Him great pleasure. So we praise God for the wonderful kindness He has poured out on us because we belong to His dearly loved Son. Eph.1: 5-6

ABBA, FATHER

I can hear you calling gently
Come and rest here in my arms
Though the storms rage all around your head
Your soul is safe from earthly harm
I embrace your invitation
I've no need to walk alone
My spirit knows your Spirit's call

I'm coming home.
It's not hard to recognize you
That voice sweet to my ears
Calls me to a place so long ago
Long before this world of tears
Your arms were strong to hold me
From before the dawn of time
I've always known you are my home
I'm coming home.

CHORUS
I say, "Abba Father, renew me"
I call, "Abba Father, restore me"
I cry, "Abba Daddy, release me
to live in your truth and walk in your light.

Christine Wyrtzen is the founder and director of Daughters of Promise, a national ministry for women. She is also a recording artist, author, speaker, and host of the nationally syndicated radio program "Daughters of Promise," heard daily on over 500 stations. Christine's passion is to awaken women to the extravagant love of God and equip them to live as children in His kingdom. She has been known for more than 24 years as a musician, now with 15 albums and one book to her credit. She's been nominated for a Dove Award and long admired for her ability to communicate to an audience. She is an artist with words, and her poetic bent is evident in whatever she touches.

Highlights of her public ministry include a song she wrote in 1980 that celebrated the release of the 60 Iranian hostages. She sang "They've Come Home" in Washington, D.C., on the eve of their homecoming and received a standing ovation. Her best known musical project is an album called "For Those Who Hurt" – a collection of songs to encourage those who suffer the hardships of life. Her voice is soothing and brings peace within the first few moments of listening.

She has been married for 29 years to Ron Wyrtzen, and they have two adult children.

Author's Note: Christine Wyrtzen has kindly offered to provide a free music CD to the readers of this book. An order form is available on the back page of the book, or you can write to:

If he could talk to us now...

What would President Ronald Reagan say?

"I believe with all my heart that standing up for America means standing up for the God who has so blessed our land. We need God's help to guide our nation through stormy seas. But we can't expect Him to protect America in a crisis if we just leave Him over on the shelf in our day-to-day living." – November 16, 1982 speech given to the U.S. Savings Association.

"The Founding Fathers believed that faith in God was the key to our being a good people and America's becoming a great nation." – October 13, 1983 remarks during a meeting with women from Christian religious groups at the White House.

"If America is to remain what God in His wisdom intended for it to be – a refuge, a safe haven for those seeking human rights – then we must once again extend the most basic human right to the most vulnerable members of the human family. We must commit ourselves to a future in which the right to life for every human being – no matter how weak, no matter how small, no matter how defenseless – is protected by our laws and public policy." – January 14, 1985 *Proclamation for National Sanctity-of-Human-Life Day.*

"Let us remember that whether we be Christian or Jew or Moslem, we are all children of Abraham, we are all children of the same God." – September 9, 1981 remarks at the White House upon the visit of Israeli Prime Minister Menachem Begin.

"The dustbin of history is littered with the remains of those countries that relied on diplomacy to secure their freedom. We must never forget . . . in the final analysis . . . that it is our military, industrial and economic strength that offers the best guarantee of peace for America in times of danger." – September 10, 1974 remarks at a reception for a congressional candidate.

"As for the enemies of freedom, those who are potential adversaries, they will be reminded that peace is the highest aspiration of the American people. We will negotiate for it, sacrifice for it; we will never surrender for it, now or ever." – January 20, 1981 *First Inaugural Address.*

"I don' know all the national anthems of the world, but I do know this: The only anthem of those I do know that ends with a question is ours, and may it ever be thus. Does that banner still wave 'o'er the land of the free and the home of the brave?' Yes it does, and we're going to see that it continues to wave over that kind of a country." – May 4, 1982 Republican Congressional "Salute to President Reagan" dinner.

HONOR ROLL

The Missing and Dead

Sadly this is only a partial list because lists by the various agencies involved are being updated daily. This list is alphabetical and contains the names of the missing and dead on all the airplanes and at each crash site September 11, 2001. This list was generated through various public reports.

Gordon McCannel Aamoth, 32, New York, N.Y.
World Trade Center

Edelmiro Abad, 55
World Trade Center

Maria Rose Abad
World Trade Center

Andrew Anthony Abate, 37, Melville, N.Y.
World Trade Center

Vincent Abate, New York, N.Y.
World Trade Center

Heinz Ackermann
World Trade Center

Paul Andrew Acquaviva, 29, Glen Rock, N.J.
World Trade Center

Christian Adams, 37, Biebelsheim, Germany
United Flight 93 - Pennsylvania, airline passenger

Donald L. Adams, 28, Chatham, N.J.
World Trade Center

Terence E. Adderley, 22
World Trade Center

Lee Adler, 48, Springfield, N.J.
World Trade Center

Daniel Afflito, 32, Wayne, N.J.
World Trade Center

Joseph Agnello
World Trade Center

David Agnes, New York, N.Y.
World Trade Center

Joao A. Aguiar, 30, N.J.
World Trade Center

Lt. Brian Ahearn
World Trade Center

Joanne Ahladiotis, 27, New York, N.Y.
World Trade Center

Godwin Ajala, 33
World Trade Center

Gertrude Alagero, 37, New York, N.Y.
World Trade Center

Andrew Alameno, 37, Westfield, N.J.
World Trade Center

Gary Albero, 39, Emerson, N.J.
World Trade Center

David Alger, 57, New York, N.Y.
World Trade Center

Edward L. Allegretto, 51, Colonia, N.J.
World Trade Center

Eric Allen, 41
World Trade Center

Joseph Ryan Allen, 38
World Trade Center

Richard Allen
World Trade Center

Christopher Edward Allingham, 36, River Edge, N.J.
World Trade Center

Anna Williams Allison, 48, Stoneham, Mass.
American Flight 11 - WTC, airline passenger

Antonio Javier Alvarez
World Trade Center

Juan Cisneros Alvarez, Escondido, Calif.
World Trade Center

Telmo Alvear, 25, New York, N.Y.
World Trade Center

Tariq Amanullah, 40, Metuchen, N.J.
World Trade Center

James Amato, 43, Ronkonkoma, N.Y.
World Trade Center

Joseph Amatuccio, New York, N.Y.
World Trade Center

Paul Ambrose, 32
American Flight 77 - Pentagon, airline passenger

Christopher Amoroso, 29, New York, N.Y.
World Trade Center

Spc. Craig Amundson, 28, Fort Belvoir, Va.
Pentagon

Calixto Anaya
World Trade Center

Joe Anchundia
World Trade Center

Kermit C. Anderson, 57, Green Brook, N.J.
World Trade Center

Michael Andrews, 34, Belle Harbor, N.Y.
World Trade Center

Jean A. Andrucki, Hoboken, N.J.
World Trade Center

Siew N. Ang, 37, East Brunswick, N.J.
World Trade Center

Joseph Angelini, 63, Lindenhurst, N.Y.
World Trade Center

Joseph Angelini
World Trade Center

David Angell, 54, Pasadena, Calif.
American Flight 11 - WTC, airline passenger

Lynn Angell, 52, Pasadena, Calif.
American Flight 11 - WTC, airline passenger

Laura Angilletta, 23, New York, N.Y.
World Trade Center

Lorraine D. Antigua, 32, Middletown, N.J.
World Trade Center

Seima Aoyama
American Flight 11 - WTC, airline passenger

Peter P. Apollo, 26, Waretown, N.J.
World Trade Center

Faustino Apostol
World Trade Center

Frank Aquilino, New York, N.Y.
World Trade Center

Patrick M. Aranyos, 26, New York, N.Y.
World Trade Center

David Arce
World Trade Center

Michael G. Arczynski, 45, Little Silver, N.J.
World Trade Center

Louis Arena, 32, New York, N.Y.
World Trade Center

Barbara Arestegui, 38, Marstons Mills, Mass.
American Flight 11 - WTC, flight crew

Adam Arias, 37, New York, N.Y.
World Trade Center

Michael J. Armstrong, 34, New York, N.Y.
World Trade Center

Josh Aron, New York, N.Y.
World Trade Center

Richard A. Aronow, Mahwah, N.J.
World Trade Center

Myra Aronson, 52, Charlestown, Mass.
American Flight 11 - WTC, airline passenger

Carl Asaro
World Trade Center

Michael A. Asciak, 47, Ridgefield, N.J.
World Trade Center

Janice Ashley
World Trade Center

Thomas J. Ashton, 21, Woodside, N.Y.
World Trade Center

Lt. Gregg Atlas
World Trade Center

Gerald Atwood
World Trade Center

Frank Louis Aversano, 58, Manalapan, N.J.
World Trade Center

Ezra Aviles, Commack, N.Y.
World Trade Center

Alona Avraham, 30, Ashdod, Israel
United Flight 175 - WTC, airline passenger

Arlene T. Babakitis, 47, Secaucus, N.J.
World Trade Center

Eustace Bacchus, 48
World Trade Center

John Badagliacca, 35, New York, N.Y.
World Trade Center

Brett T. Bailey, 28, Brick, N.J.
World Trade Center

Garnet Bailey, 53, Lynnfield, Mass.
United Flight 175 - WTC, airline passenger

Julio Minto Balanca
World Trade Center

Michael Andrew Bane, 33, Yardley, Pa.
World Trade Center

Gerard Baptiste
World Trade Center

Gerard A. Barbara, 53, West Brighton, N.Y.
World Trade Center

Paul V. Barbaro, 35, Holmdel, N.J.
World Trade Center

James W. Barbella, Oceanside, N.Y.
World Trade Center

Christine Barbuto, 32, Brookline, Mass.
American Flight 11 - WTC, airline passenger

Colleen A. Barkow, 26, East Windsor, N.J.
World Trade Center

Matthew Barnes
World Trade Center

Melissa Rose Barnes, 27, Redlands, Calif.
Pentagon

Sheila Barnes, 55
World Trade Center

Evan J. Baron, 38, Bridgewater, N.J.
World Trade Center

Arthur Barry
World Trade Center

Maurice Barry, 48, Rutherford, N.J.
World Trade Center

Carlton W. Bartels, New York, N.Y.
World Trade Center

Inna Basina, 43, New York, N.Y.
World Trade Center

Alysia Basmajian, 23, Bayonne, N.J.
World Trade Center

Lt. Steven Bates
World Trade Center

David Bauer, 45, Rumson, N.J.
World Trade Center

Marlyn Bautista, 46, Iselin, N.J.
World Trade Center

Mark Bavis, 31, West Newton, Mass.
United Flight 175 - WTC, airline passenger

Lorraine G. Bay, Hightstown, N.J.
United Flight 93 - Pennsylvania, flight crew

Todd Beamer, 32, Cranbury, N.J.
United Flight 93 - Pennsylvania, airline passenger

Paul Beatini, 40, Park Ridge, N.J.
World Trade Center

Jane S. Beatty, 53, Belford, N.J.
World Trade Center

Alan Beaven, 48, Oakland, Calif.
United Flight 93 - Pennsylvania, airline passenger

Larry Beck, Baldwin, N.Y.
World Trade Center

Manette Beckles, 43, Rahway, N.J.
World Trade Center

Carl Bedigian
World Trade Center

Michael Beekman, 39
World Trade Center

Maria Behr, 41, Milford, N.J.
World Trade Center

(Retired) Master Sgt. Max Beilke, 69, Laurel, Md.
Pentagon

Helen Belilovsky
World Trade Center

Debbie S. Bellows, 30, East Windsor, N.J.
World Trade Center

Stephen Belson
World Trade Center

Paul Benedetti, 32
World Trade Center

Denise Benedetto, 40
World Trade Center

Bryan C. Bennett, 25, New York, N.Y.
World Trade Center

Eric Bennett, 29
World Trade Center

Margaret L. Benson, 52, Rockaway, N.J.
World Trade Center

Dominick J. Berardi, 25, Whitestone, N.Y.
World Trade Center

Jim Berger, 44
World Trade Center

Steven H. Berger, 45, Manalapan, N.J.
World Trade Center

John Bergin
World Trade Center

Alvin Bergsohn, 48, Baldwin Harbor, N.Y.
World Trade Center

Daniel Bergstein, Teaneck, N.J.
World Trade Center

Graham Berkeley, 37, Wellesley, Mass.
United Flight 175 - WTC, airline passenger

Donna Bernaerts-Kearns, 44, Hoboken, N.J.
World Trade Center

William Bernstein, 44, New York, N.Y.
World Trade Center

David S. Berry, 43, New York, N.Y.
World Trade Center

Joseph Berry, Saddle River, N.J.
World Trade Center

William R. Bethke, 36, Hamilton, N.J.
World Trade Center

Yeneneh Betru, 35, Burbank, Calif.
American Flight 77 - Pentagon, airline passenger

Timothy D. Betterly, 42, Little Silver, N.J.
World Trade Center

Carolyn Beug, 48, Los Angeles, Calif.
American Flight 11 - WTC, airline passenger

Paul Beyer
World Trade Center

Anil Bharvaney, 41, East Windsor, N.J.
World Trade Center

Bella Bhukan, 24, Union, N.J.
World Trade Center

Peter Bielfeld
World Trade Center

William Biggart, 54, New York, N.Y.
World Trade Center

Brian Bilcher
World Trade Center

Mark Bingham, 31, San Francisco, Calif.
United Flight 93 - Pennsylvania, airline passenger

Carl Bini
World Trade Center

Gary Bird, 51, Tempe, Ariz.
World Trade Center

Joshua David Birnbaum, 24, New York, N.Y.
World Trade Center

George John Bishop, 52, Granite Springs, N.Y.
World Trade Center

Kris Romeo Bishundat, 23, Waldorf, Md.
Pentagon

Jeffrey D. Bittner, 27
World Trade Center

Christopher Blackwell
World Trade Center

Carrie Blagburn, 48, Temple Hills, Md.
Pentagon

Susan Blair, 35
World Trade Center

Harry Blanding, 38
World Trade Center

Richard M. Blood, 38, Ridgewood, N.J.
World Trade Center

Mike Boccardi
World Trade Center

John P. Bocchi, 38, New Vernon, N.J.
World Trade Center

Michael Bocchino
World Trade Center

Susan Bochino, 36
World Trade Center

Deora Bodley, 20, Santa Clara, Calif.
United Flight 93 - Pennsylvania, airline passenger

Bruce (Chappy) Boehm, 49, West Hempstead, N.Y.
World Trade Center

Mary Boffa, 45, New York, N.Y.
World Trade Center

Nicholas A. Bogdan, 33, Pemberton, N.J.
World Trade Center

Darren Bohan, 34
World Trade Center

Lawrence F. Boisseau, 36, Freehold, N.J.
World Trade Center

Vincent Boland, 25, N.J.
World Trade Center

Touri Bolourchi, 69, Beverly Hills, Calif.
United Flight 175 - WTC, airline passenger

Alan Bondarenko, 53, Flemington, N.J.
World Trade Center

Colin Bonnett, 23
World Trade Center

Frank Bonomo
World Trade Center

Sean Booker, 35, Newark, N.J.
World Trade Center

Kelly Booms, 24, Boston, Mass.
American Flight 11 - WTC, airline passenger

Lt. Col. Canfield D. Boone, 54, Clifton, Va.
Pentagon

MJ Booth
American Flight 77 - Pentagon, airline passenger

Juan Jose Borda Leyva, 59, New York, N.Y.
World Trade Center, Colombian

Sherry Bordeaux, 38, Jersey City, N.J.
World Trade Center

Krystine C. Bordenabe, 33, Old Bridge, N.J.
World Trade Center

Richard E. Bosco, 34, Suffern, N.Y.
World Trade Center

Klaus Bothe, 31
United Flight 175 - WTC, airline passenger

Carol Bouchard, 43, Warwick, R.I.
American Flight 11 - WTC, airline passenger

J. Howard Boulton
World Trade Center

Thomas H. Bowden, 36, Wyckoff, N.J.
World Trade Center

Donna Bowen, 42
Pentagon

Shawn Edward Bowman, 29, New York, N.Y.
World Trade Center

Gary Box
World Trade Center

Gennady Boyarsky, 45
World Trade Center

Pamela Boyce, 43, New York, N.Y.
World Trade Center

Allen Boyle, 30, Fredericksburg, Va.
Pentagon

Michael Boyle
World Trade Center

Alfred Braca, 54, Leonardo, N.J.
World Trade Center

Kevin Bracken
World Trade Center

Sandra W. Bradshaw, 38, Greensboro, N.C.
United Flight 93 - Pennsylvania, flight crew

David Brady, Summit, N.J.
World Trade Center

Alex Braginsky, 38, Stamford, Conn.
World Trade Center

Nicholas Brandemarti, 21, Mantua, N.J.
World Trade Center

Daniel Brandhorst, 42, Los Angeles, Calif.
United Flight 175 - WTC, airline passenger

David Brandhorst, 3, Los Angeles, Calif.
United Flight 175 - WTC, airline passenger

Michelle Renee Bratton, 23, Yonkers, N.Y.
World Trade Center

Patrice Braut
World Trade Center, Belgian

Lydia E. Bravo, 50, Dunellen, N.J.
World Trade Center

Ronald Breitweiser, 39, Navesink, N.J.
World Trade Center

Edward A. Brennan, 37, N.J.
World Trade Center

Frank Brennan, 50, Oak Beach, N.Y.
World Trade Center

Michael Brennan
World Trade Center

Peter Brennan, 30, Ronkonkoma, N.Y.
World Trade Center

Tom Brennan
World Trade Center

Capt. Daniel Brethel, 40
World Trade Center

Jonathan Briley, 43
World Trade Center

Marion Britton, 53
United Flight 93 - Pennsylvania, airline passenger

Mark F. Broderick, 42, Old Bridge, N.J.
World Trade Center

Herman Broghammer, 58
World Trade Center

Keith Broomfield, 49
World Trade Center

Bernard Brown, 11
American Flight 77 - Pentagon, airline passenger

Capt. Patrick Brown
World Trade Center

Mark Bruce, 40
World Trade Center

Andrew Brunn, 28
World Trade Center

Capt. Vincent Brunton
World Trade Center

Ronald Bucca
World Trade Center

Eustice Buccus, 48, N.J.
World Trade Center

Greg Buck
World Trade Center

Dennis Buckley, 38, Chatham, N.J.
World Trade Center

Nancy Bueche, 43
World Trade Center

Patrick J. Buhse, 36, Lincroft, N.J.
World Trade Center

John E. Bulaga, 35, Paterson, N.J.
World Trade Center

Stephen Bunin, 45
World Trade Center

Christopher Lee Burford, 23, Hubert, N.C.
Pentagon

Matthew Burke, 28, New York, N.Y.
World Trade Center

Thomas Daniel Burke, 38, Bedford Hills, N.Y.
World Trade Center

Capt. William Burke
World Trade Center

Charles Burlingame, 51, Herndon, Va.
American Flight 77 - Pentagon, flight crew

Thomas E. Burnett, 38, San Ramon, Calif.
United Flight 93 - Pennsylvania, airline passenger

Donald Burns
World Trade Center

Keith Burns, 39, East Rutherford, N.J.
World Trade Center

John Burnside
World Trade Center

Milton Bustillo, 37
World Trade Center, Colombian

Thomas Butler
World Trade Center

Patrick Byrne
World Trade Center

Timothy G. Byrne, 36
World Trade Center

Daniel Martin Caballero, 21, Houston, Texas
Pentagon

Lillian Caceres, 48
World Trade Center

Steven Cafiero, 31, New York, N.Y.
World Trade Center

John Cahill, 56, Wellesley, Mass.
United Flight 175 - WTC, airline passenger

Michael Cahill, East Williston, N.Y.
World Trade Center

Scott Cahill, 30, West Caldwell, N.J.
World Trade Center

George Cain
World Trade Center

Salvatore Calabro
World Trade Center

Edward Calderon, 43, Jersey City, N.J.
World Trade Center

Sgt. First Class Jose Calderon, 44, Puerto Rico
Pentagon

Dominick Calia, 40, Manalapan, N.J.
World Trade Center

Capt. Frank Callahan
World Trade Center

Liam Callahan, Rockaway, N.J.
World Trade Center

Suzanne Calley, 42, San Martin, Calif.
American Flight 77 - Pentagon, airline passenger

Luigi Calvi, 34, East Rutherford, N.J.
World Trade Center

Michael Cammarata, 22, Huguenot, N.Y.
World Trade Center

David Campbell, 51, Basking Ridge, N.J.
World Trade Center

Geoff Campbell
World Trade Center

Juan Ortega Campos
World Trade Center

John A. Candela, 42, Glen Ridge, N.J.
World Trade Center

Vincent Cangelosi, 30, New York, N.Y.
World Trade Center

Stephen J. Cangialosi, 40, Middletown, N.J.
World Trade Center

Lisa Cannava
World Trade Center

Brian Cannizzaro
World Trade Center

Michael R. Canty, 30
World Trade Center

Louis A. Caporicci, 35, Tottenville, N.Y.
World Trade Center

Jonathan N. Cappello, Garden City, N.Y.
World Trade Center

Richard Caproni, 34, Lynbrook, N.Y.
World Trade Center

Jose Cardona
World Trade Center

Dennis Carey, 51
World Trade Center

Michael Carlo
World Trade Center

David Carlone, 46, Randolph, N.J.
World Trade Center

Jeremy M. Carrington, 34, New York, N.Y.
World Trade Center

Michael Carroll
World Trade Center

Peter Carroll, 35
World Trade Center

Christoffer Carstanjen, 33, Turner Falls, Mass.
United Flight 175 - WTC, airline passenger

Angelene C. Carter, 51, Forrestville, Md.
Pentagon

Christopher Newton Carter, 52, Middletown, N.J.
World Trade Center

Sharon Carver, 38, Md.
Pentagon

Paul Cascio, 23, Manhasset, N.Y.
World Trade Center

Kathleen Hunt Casey, 43, Middletown, N.J.
World Trade Center

Neilie Casey, 32, Wellesley, Mass.
American Flight 11 - WTC, airline passenger

William Cashman
United Flight 93 - Pennsylvania, airline passenger

Margarito Casillas
World Trade Center

Thomas Casoria
World Trade Center

William O. Caspar, 57, Eatontown, N.J.
World Trade Center

Alejandro Castano, 35
World Trade Center, Colombian

Leonard M. Castrianno, 30, New York, N.Y.
World Trade Center

William E. Caswell, 54, Silver Spring, Md.
American Flight 77 - Pentagon, airline passenger

Robert J. Caufield, 49, Valley Stream, N.Y.
World Trade Center

Judson Cavalier
World Trade Center

Michael Cawley
World Trade Center

Jason D. Cayne, 33, Morganville, N.J.
World Trade Center

Marcia G. Cecil
World Trade Center

Juan Cevallos, 44
World Trade Center

John J. Chada, 55, Manassas, Va.
Pentagon

Jeffrey M. Chairnoff, 17, N.J.
World Trade Center

Rosa Maria (Rosemary) Chapa, Springfield, Va.
Pentagon

Mark Charette, 38, Millburn, N.J.
World Trade Center

David M. Charlebois, 39, Washington, D.C.
American Flight 77 - Pentagon, flight crew

Pedro Francisco Checo, 35
World Trade Center, Colombian

Douglas MacMillan Cherry, 38, Maplewood, N.J.
World Trade Center

Stephen P. Cherry, 41, Stamford, Conn.
World Trade Center

Vernon Cherry
World Trade Center

Nestor Chevalier, 30, New York, N.Y.
World Trade Center

Swede Joseph Chevalier, 26, Locust, N.J.
World Trade Center

Dorothy J. Chiarchiaro, 61, Vernon, N.J.
World Trade Center

Robert Chin, 33, New York, N.Y.
World Trade Center

Nicholas Chiofalo
World Trade Center

John Chipura
World Trade Center

Catherine E. Chirls, Princeton, N.J.
World Trade Center

Kaccy Cho, 30
World Trade Center

Kirsten L. Christophe, 39, Maplewood, N.J.
World Trade Center

Pamela Chu, New York, N.Y.
World Trade Center

Steven P. Chucknick, 44, Cliffwood Beach, N.J.
World Trade Center

Wai Chung, 36
World Trade Center

Christopher Ciafardini, 30
World Trade Center

Alex Ciccone, 38, New Rochelle, N.Y.
World Trade Center

Lt. Robert Cirri, 39, Nutley, N.J.
World Trade Center

Eugene Clark, 47
World Trade Center

Gregory Clark, 40, Teaneck, N.J.
World Trade Center

Sarah Clark, 65, Columbia, Md.
American Flight 77 - Pentagon, airline passenger

Tom Clark
World Trade Center

Christopher Robert Clarke, 34, Philadelphia, Pa.
World Trade Center

Michael Clarke
World Trade Center

Kevin F. Cleary, 38
World Trade Center

Jim Cleere, 55, Newton, Iowa
World Trade Center

Nestor Clinton, 26
World Trade Center

Geoffrey Cloud, 36, Stamford, Conn.
World Trade Center

Steven Coakley
World Trade Center

Patricia A. Cody, 46, Brigantine, N.J.
World Trade Center

Daniel Michael Coffey, 54, Newburgh, N.Y.
World Trade Center

Jason Matthew Coffey, 25, Newburgh, N.Y.
World Trade Center

Kevin Cohen, 28, Metuchen, N.J.
World Trade Center

Mark Colaio
World Trade Center

Stephen J. Colaio, 32, Montauk, N.Y.
World Trade Center

Christopher Colasanti, 33, Hoboken, N.J.
World Trade Center

Kevin N. Colbert, West Hempstead, N.Y.
World Trade Center

Keith E. Coleman, 34, Warren, N.J.
World Trade Center

Tarel Coleman
World Trade Center

Robert Colin, 49
World Trade Center

Robert J. Coll, 35, Glen Ridge, N.J.
World Trade Center

Jean M. Collin, 42
World Trade Center

John Collins, 42, New York, N.Y.
World Trade Center

Michael Collins, 38, Montclair, N.J.
World Trade Center

Thomas J. Collins, 36, New York, N.Y.
World Trade Center

Jeffrey Collman, 41, Novato, Calif.
American Flight 11 - WTC, flight crew

Linda M. Colon, 46, Perrineville, N.J.
World Trade Center

Denease Conley, 43, New York, N.Y.
World Trade Center

Susan Clancy Conlon, New York, N.Y.
World Trade Center

Cynthia L. Connolly, 30, Metuchen, N.J.
World Trade Center

John E. Connolly, 46, Wall, N.J.
World Trade Center

James Lee Connor, 38, Summit, N.J.
World Trade Center

J.C. Connors, 65, New York, N.Y.
World Trade Center

Kevin P. Connors, 55, Greenwich, Conn.
World Trade Center

Dennis Michael Cook, 33, Marlboro, N.J.
World Trade Center

Jeffrey Coombs, 42, Abington, Mass.
American Flight 11 - WTC, airline passenger

James L. Cooper, 46, Wall, N.J.
World Trade Center

John Cooper, 30, Bayonne, N.J.
World Trade Center

Julian Cooper, 39, Springdale, Md.
Pentagon

Zandra Cooper, Annandale, Va.
American Flight 77 - Pentagon, airline passenger

Joseph Coppo, 47, New Canaan, Conn.
World Trade Center

Gerard Coppola, 46, New Providence, N.J.
World Trade Center

Joseph A. Corbett, 28, Islip, N.Y.
World Trade Center

John "Jay" Corcoran, 44, Norwell, Mass.
United Flight 175 - WTC, airline passenger

Robert Cordice
World Trade Center

Daniel Correa, 25, Fairview, N.J.
World Trade Center

Ruben Correa
World Trade Center

Georgine Rose Corrigan
United Flight 93 - Pennsylvania, airline passenger

Carlos Cortes, 57, New York, N.Y.
World Trade Center

Kevin M. Cosgrove, 46, West Islip, N.Y.
World Trade Center

Dolores Costa
World Trade Center

Charles G. Costello, 46, Old Bridge, N.J.
World Trade Center

Michael Costello, Seaford, N.Y.
World Trade Center

Asia Cottom, 11
American Flight 77 - Pentagon, airline passenger

Conrod K Cottoy
World Trade Center

Martin Coughlan, 54
World Trade Center

Timothy John Coughlin, 42, New York, N.Y.
World Trade Center

Fred Cox, 27
World Trade Center

James Coyle
World Trade Center

Christopher S. Cramer, 34, Manahawkin, N.J.
World Trade Center

Lt. Cmdr. Eric Allen Cranford, 32, Drexel, N.C.
Pentagon

James Crawford, New Vernon, N.J.
World Trade Center

Robert Crawford
World Trade Center

Tara Creamer, 30, Worcester, Mass.
American Flight 11 - WTC, airline passenger

Joanne Cregan, New York, N.Y.
World Trade Center

John Crisci, 48
World Trade Center

Dennis Cross, 60, Islip Terrace, N.Y.
World Trade Center

Kevin R. Crotty, 43, Summit, N.J.
World Trade Center

Thomas G. Crotty, 42, Rockville Centre, N.Y.
World Trade Center

John Crowe, 57, Rutherford, N.J.
World Trade Center

Welles Crowther, 24, New York, N.Y.
World Trade Center

Robert L. Cruikshank, 64, New York, N.Y.
World Trade Center

John R. Cruz, 32, Lakewood, N.J.
World Trade Center

Kenneth Cubas, 48, New York, N.Y.
World Trade Center

Thelma Cuccinello, 71, Wilmot, N.H.
American Flight 11 - WTC, airline passenger

Richard Joseph Cudina, 46, Glen Gardner, N.J.
World Trade Center

Thomas P. Cullen, 31, New York, N.Y.
World Trade Center

Joan McConnell Cullinan, 47, Scarsdale, N.Y.
World Trade Center

Joan McConnell Cullinan, Scarsdale, N.Y.
World Trade Center

Joyce Cummings, 65
World Trade Center

Brian T. Cummins, 38, Manasquan, N.J.
World Trade Center

Michael J. Cunningham, 39, West Windsor, N.J.
World Trade Center

Robert Curatolo, 31
World Trade Center

Laurence Curia, 41, Garden City, N.Y.
World Trade Center

Paul Curioli, 51, Norwalk, Conn.
World Trade Center

Patrick Currivan, 52, Winchester, Mass.
American Flight 11 - WTC, airline passenger

Patricia Cushing, 69, Bayonne, N.J.
United Flight 93 - Pennsylvania, airline passenger

Gavin Cushny, 47, Hoboken, N.J.
World Trade Center

Caleb A. Dack, 39, Montclair, N.J.
World Trade Center

Carlos S. DaCosta, 41, Elizabeth, N.J.
World Trade Center, Portugese

Jason Dahl, 43, Denver, Colo.
United Flight 93 - Pennsylvania, flight crew

Brian P. Dale, 43, Warren, N.J.
American Flight 11 - WTC, airline passenger

Vincent D'Amadeo, 36, East Patchouge, N.Y.
World Trade Center

Thomas A. Damaskinos, 33, Allendale, N.J.
World Trade Center

Jack L. D'Ambrosi, 45, Woodcliff Lake, N.J.
World Trade Center

Jeannine Damiani-Jones, 28, New York, N.Y.
World Trade Center

Patrick W. Danahy, 35, Yorktown Heights, N.Y.
World Trade Center

Dwight Donald Darcy, 55, New York, N.Y.
World Trade Center

Lt. Edward Datri
World Trade Center

Michael Dauria
World Trade Center

Lawrence Davidson, 51
World Trade Center

Michael A. Davidson, 27, Westfield, N.J.
World Trade Center

Scott Davidson
World Trade Center

Niurka Davila, New York, N.Y.
World Trade Center

Ada Davis, 57, Camp Springs, Md.
Pentagon

Clinton Davis, 38
World Trade Center

Wayne T. Davis, 29
World Trade Center

Calvin Dawson
World Trade Center

Edward Day
World Trade Center

Gloria de Barrera, 49, El Salvador
World Trade Center

Azucena de la Torre, 50, New York, N.Y.
World Trade Center

Cristina de Laura
World Trade Center, Colombian

Oscar de Laura
World Trade Center, Colombian

Frank A. De Martini, New York, N.Y.
World Trade Center

Robert J. DeAngelis
World Trade Center

Thomas Deangelis
World Trade Center

Dorothy Dearaujo, 82, Long Beach, Calif.
United Flight 175 - WTC, airline passenger

James Debeuneure, 58, Upper Marlboro, Md.
American Flight 77 - Pentagon, airline passenger

James V. Deblase, 45, Manalapan, N.J.
World Trade Center

Capt. Gerald Francis Deconto, 44, Sandwich, Mass.
Pentagon

David Defeo
World Trade Center

Nereida DeJesus, 30
World Trade Center

Donald A. Delapenha, 37, Allendale, N.J.
World Trade Center

Joseph Della Pietra, 24, New York, N.Y.
World Trade Center

Colleen Deloughery, 41, Bayonne, N.J.
World Trade Center

Joseph Deluca, 52, Ledgewood, N.J.
United Flight 93 - Pennsylvania, airline passenger

Manuel DelValle, New York, N.Y.
World Trade Center

Anthony Demas, New York, N.Y.
World Trade Center

Martin Demeo, 47
World Trade Center

Francis X. Deming, 47, Franklin Lakes, N.J.
World Trade Center

Kevin Dennis, 43, Peapack, N.J.
World Trade Center

Thomas Dennis, 37, Franklin Lakes, N.J.
World Trade Center

David Derubbio
World Trade Center

Jayceryll M. Deschavez, 24, Carteret, N.J.
World Trade Center

Christian L. DeSimone, 23, Ringwood, N.J.
World Trade Center

Lt. Andrew Desperito, 44, Patchogue, N.Y.
World Trade Center

Michael J. Desposito, 32, Morganville, N.J.
World Trade Center

Cindy Deuel
World Trade Center

Jerry DeVito
World Trade Center

Robert P. Devitt, 36, Plainsboro, N.J.
World Trade Center

Dennis Devlin, 51, Washingtonville, N.Y.
World Trade Center

Gerard Dewan
World Trade Center

Simon Dhanani, 63
World Trade Center

Debra A. Di Martino
World Trade Center

Michael DiAgostino
World Trade Center

Lourdes Galleti Diaz, 32
World Trade Center

Michael Diaz-Piedra, 49
World Trade Center

Rodney Dickens, 11
American Flight 77 - Pentagon, airline passenger

Lt. Col. Jerry D. Dickerson, 41, Miss.
Pentagon

Joseph D. Dickey, 50, Manhasset, N.Y.
World Trade Center

Lawrence P. Dickinson, 35, Morganville, N.J.
World Trade Center

Michael D. Diehl, 48, Brick, N.J.
World Trade Center

Vincent F. Difazio, 43, Hampton, N.J.
World Trade Center

Eddie Dillard
American Flight 77 - Pentagon, airline passenger

David DiMeglio, Wakefield, Mass.
American Flight 11 - WTC, airline passenger

Stephen P. Dimino, 48, Basking Ridge, N.J.
World Trade Center

Christopher Dincuff, 31, Jersey City, N.J.
World Trade Center

Anthony DiOnisio, 38, Glen Rock, N.J.
World Trade Center

George Dipasquale
World Trade Center

Douglas F. DiStefano, 24, Hoboken, N.J.
World Trade Center

Donald Ditullio, 49, Peabody, Mass.
American Flight 11 - WTC, airline passenger

Ramzi Doany, 35, Bayonne, N.J.
World Trade Center

Johnnie Doctor, 32, Jacksonville, Fla.
Pentagon

John J. Doherty, Hartsdale, N.Y.
World Trade Center

Brendan Dolan, 37, Glen Rock, N.J.
World Trade Center

Capt. Robert Edward Dolan, 43, Florham Park, N.J.
Pentagon

Neil Dollard, 28, New York, N.Y.
World Trade Center

Albert Dominguez, 65, Sydney, Australia
American Flight 11 - WTC, airline passenger

Geronimo Dominguez
World Trade Center

Lt. Kevin Donnelly
World Trade Center

Jacqueline Donovan, 34
World Trade Center

Cmdr. William Howard Donovan, 37, Nunda, N.Y.
Pentagon

Steven S. Dorf, 39, N.J.
World Trade Center

Thomas Dowd, 37, Monroe, N.Y.
World Trade Center

Lt. Kevin Dowdell
World Trade Center

Yolanda Dowling
World Trade Center

Ray Downey
World Trade Center

Frank J. Doyle
World Trade Center

Joseph Doyle, New York, N.Y.
World Trade Center

Randy Drake, 37, Lee's Summit, Mo.
World Trade Center

Patrick Driscoll
United Flight 93 - Pennsylvania, airline passenger

Charles Droz, 52, Springfield, Va.
American Flight 77 - Pentagon, airline passenger

Luke A. Dudek, 50, Livingston, N.J.
World Trade Center

Christopher Michael Duffy, 23, New York, N.Y.
World Trade Center

Gerard Duffy
World Trade Center

Michael Joseph Duffy, 29, New York, N.Y.
World Trade Center

Antoinette Duger, 44, Glen Gardner, N.J.
World Trade Center

Cmdr. Patrick S. Dunn, 39, Fords, N.J.
Pentagon

Richard Dunstan, 54, New Providence, N.J.
World Trade Center

Joseph Anthony Eacobacci, 26, New York, N.Y.
World Trade Center

Bruce Eagleson, 53, Middlefield, Conn.
World Trade Center

Edward Thomas Earhart, 26, Salt Lick, Ky.
Pentagon

Robert Eaton
World Trade Center

Dean Eberling, 44, Cranford, N.J.
World Trade Center

Paul R. Eckna, 38, West New York, N.J.
World Trade Center

Gus Economos
World Trade Center

Barbara G. Edwards, 58, Las Vegas, Nev.
American Flight 77 - Pentagon, airline passenger

Dennis M. Edwards, 35, Huntington, N.Y.
World Trade Center

Mike Edwards
World Trade Center

Christine Egan, 55
World Trade Center

Lisa Egan, 31, Cliffside Park, N.J.
World Trade Center

Capt. Martin Egan, 36, New York, N.Y.
World Trade Center

Michael Egan, 51
World Trade Center

Samantha Egan, 24, Jersey City, N.J.
World Trade Center

Lisa Caren Ehrlich, 36, New York, N.Y.
World Trade Center

Michael Elferis
World Trade Center

Valerie Silver Ellis
World Trade Center

Albert A. Elmarry, 30, North Brunswick, N.J.
World Trade Center

Lt. Cmdr. Robert Randolph Elseth, 37, Vestal, N.Y.
Pentagon

Edgar Emery, 45, Clifton, N.J.
World Trade Center

Ulf R. Ericson, 79, Greenwich, Conn.
World Trade Center

Erwin Erke, 41, Farmingdale, N.Y.
World Trade Center

William J. Erwin, 30, Verona, N.J.
World Trade Center

Fanny M. Espinoza, 29, Teaneck, N.J.
World Trade Center

Francis Esposito
World Trade Center

Lt. Michael Esposito
World Trade Center

William Esposito
World Trade Center

Ruben Esquilin, 35, New York, N.Y.
World Trade Center

Barbara Etzold, 43, Jersey City, N.J.
World Trade Center

Eric Evans, 31, Norwich, Conn.
World Trade Center

Robert Evans
World Trade Center

John Fabian, 57, North Bergen, N.J.
World Trade Center

Patricia M. Fagan, 55, Toms River, N.J.
World Trade Center

Charles S. Falkenberg, 45, University Park, Md.
American Flight 77 - Pentagon, airline passenger

Dana Falkenberg, 3, University Park, Md.
American Flight 77 - Pentagon, airline passenger

Zoe Falkenberg, 8, University Park, Md.
American Flight 77 - Pentagon, airline passenger

Jamie Lynn Fallon, 23, Woodbridge, Va.
Pentagon

William F. Fallon, 53, Rocky Hill, N.J.
World Trade Center

Robert Fangman, 33, Claymont, Del.
United Flight 175 - WTC, flight crew

John Fanning
World Trade Center

Capt. Thomas Farino
World Trade Center

Betty Farmer, 62, New York, N.Y.
World Trade Center

John W. Farrell, 41, Basking Ridge, N.J.
World Trade Center

Terrence Farrell
World Trade Center

Capt. Joseph Farrelly
World Trade Center

Christopher Faughnan, 37, South Orange, N.J.
World Trade Center

Wendy Faulkner, 47, Mason, Ohio
World Trade Center

Ronald Fazio, 57, Closter, N.J.
World Trade Center

William Feehan, 72, New York, N.Y.
World Trade Center

Sean Fegan, 34, New York, N.Y.
World Trade Center

Lee Fehling
World Trade Center

Alan Feinberg, 48, Marlboro, N.J.
World Trade Center

Edward P. Felt, 41, Matawan, N.J.
United Flight 93 - Pennsylvania, airline passenger

Edward T. Fergus, 40, Wilton, Conn.
World Trade Center

George Ferguson, 54, Teaneck, N.J.
World Trade Center

James Joe Ferguson, 39, Washington, D.C.
American Flight 77 - Pentagon, airline passenger

Henry Fernandez
World Trade Center

Jose Manuel Contreras Fernandez
World Trade Center

Judy H. Fernandez, 27, Parlin, N.J.
World Trade Center

Julio Fernandez Ramirez, 47
World Trade Center, Peruvian

David Ferrugio, 46, Middletown, N.J.
World Trade Center

Louis V. Fersini, 39, Basking Ridge, N.J.
World Trade Center

Mike Ferugio
World Trade Center

Brad Fetchet, 24, New York, N.Y.
World Trade Center

Jennifer L. Fialko, 29, Teaneck, N.J.
World Trade Center

Amelia V. Fields, 36, Dumfries, Va.
Pentagon

Alex Filipov, 70, Concord, Mass.
American Flight 11 - WTC, airline passenger

Michael Bradley Finnegan, 37, Basking Ridge, N.J.
World Trade Center

Timothy J. Finnerty, 33, Glen Rock, N.J.
World Trade Center

Michael Fiore
World Trade Center

Stephen J. Fiorelli, 43, Aberdeen, N.J.
World Trade Center

Paul Fiori, 31, Yorktown Heights, N.Y.
World Trade Center

John Fiorito, 40, Stamford, Conn.
World Trade Center

Lt. John Fischer
World Trade Center

Bennett Lawson Fisher, 58, Stamford, Conn.
World Trade Center

Gerald P. Fisher, 57, Potomac, Md.
Pentagon

John R. Fisher, 46, Bayonne, N.J.
World Trade Center

Thomas J. Fisher, 36, Union, N.J.
World Trade Center

Lucy Fishman
World Trade Center

Tom Fitzpatrick
World Trade Center

Sal A. Fiumefreddo, 47, Manalapan, N.J.
World Trade Center

Darlene Flagg, 63, Millwood, Va.
American Flight 77 - Pentagon, airline passenger

Wilson Flagg, 63, Millwood, Va.
American Flight 77 - Pentagon, airline passenger

(Donovan) Christina Flannery
World Trade Center

Andre Fletcher
World Trade Center

Carl Flickinger, 38, Conyers, N.Y.
World Trade Center

Matthew Michael Flocco, 21, Newark, Del.
Pentagon

John Florio
World Trade Center

Joseph W. Flounders
World Trade Center

Carol Flyzik, 40, Plaistow, N.H.
American Flight 11 - WTC, airline passenger

David Fodor, 38, Garrison, N.Y.
World Trade Center

Lt. Michael Fodor
World Trade Center

Steven Fogel, Westfield, N.Y.
World Trade Center

Thomas Foley, 32, West Nyack, N.Y.
World Trade Center

Jane Folger, 73, Bayonne, N.J.
United Flight 93 - Pennsylvania, airline passenger

David Fontana
World Trade Center

Dennis Foo, 30, Holmdel, N.J.
World Trade Center

Bobby Forbes, 37, N.J.
World Trade Center

Donald Foreman, New York, N.Y.
World Trade Center

Christopher H. Forsythe, 44, Basking Ridge, N.J.
World Trade Center

Claudia Foster, 26, New York, N.Y.
World Trade Center

Noel J. Foster, 40, Bridgewater, N.J.
World Trade Center

Sandra N. Foster, 41, Clinton, Md.
Pentagon

Robert Foti
World Trade Center

Jeffrey L. Fox, 40, Cranbury, N.J.
World Trade Center

Pauline Francis
World Trade Center

Gary J. Frank, 35, South Amboy, N.J.
World Trade Center

Morty Frank
World Trade Center

Peter Christopher Frank, 29, Great Neck, N.Y.
World Trade Center

Colleen Fraser, 51, Elizabeth, N.J.
United Flight 93 - Pennsylvania, airline passenger

Richard K. Fraser, 32, New York, N.Y.
World Trade Center

Kevin Joseph Frawley, 34, Yonkers, N.Y.
World Trade Center

Lillian I. Frederick, 46, Teaneck, N.J.
World Trade Center

Andrew Fredericks
World Trade Center

Brett O. Freiman, 29
World Trade Center

Lt. Peter Freund
World Trade Center

Arlene Fried, Roslyn Heights, N.Y.
World Trade Center

Andrew Friedman, Woodbury, N.Y.
World Trade Center

Paul Friedman, 45, Belmont, Mass.
American Flight 11 - WTC, airline passenger

Gregg J. Froehner, 46, Chester, N.J.
World Trade Center

Lisa Frost, 22, Rancho Santa Margarita, Calif.
United Flight 175 - WTC, airline passenger

Peter C. Fry, 36, Wilton, Conn.
World Trade Center

Paul James Furmato, 37, Colts Neck, N.J.
World Trade Center

Karleton D.B. Fyfe, 31, Brookline, Mass.
American Flight 11 - WTC, airline passenger

Richard P. Gabriel, 54, Great Falls, Va.
American Flight 77 - Pentagon, airline passenger

Pamela Gaff, 51
World Trade Center

Grace Galante, 29, New York, N.Y.
World Trade Center

Anthony E. Gallagher, 41
World Trade Center

Daniel J. Gallagher, 23, Red Bank, N.J.
World Trade Center

John Gallagher
World Trade Center

Cono E. Gallo
World Trade Center

Vincenzo Gallucci, Jamesburg, N.J.
World Trade Center

Thomas Edward Galvin, 32, New York, N.Y.
World Trade Center

Giovanna (Genni) Gambale, 27, New York, N.Y.
World Trade Center

Thomas Gambino
World Trade Center

Ronald Gamboa, 33, Los Angeles, Calif.
United Flight 175 - WTC, airline passenger

Peter J. Ganci, 55, North Massapequa, N.Y.
World Trade Center

Michael Gann, 41, Roswell, Ga.
World Trade Center

Lt. Charles Garbarini
World Trade Center

Andrew Garcia, 62, Portola Valley, Calif.
United Flight 93 - Pennsylvania, airline passenger

Douglas B. Gardner
World Trade Center

Harvey J. Gardner, 35, Lakewood, N.J.
World Trade Center

Jeffrey Gardner, 36, Hoboken, N.J.
World Trade Center

Thomas Gardner
World Trade Center

William Gardner
World Trade Center

James Gartenberg, 36
World Trade Center

Matthew Garvey
World Trade Center

Bruce Gary
World Trade Center

Donald Gavagan, New York, N.Y.
World Trade Center

Peter Gay, 54, Tewksbury, Mass.
American Flight 11 - WTC, airline passenger

Gary Geidel
World Trade Center

Paul Hamilton Geier, 36, Farmingdale, N.Y.
World Trade Center

Julie Geis, 44, Lees Summit, Mo.
World Trade Center

Peter Gelinas, 34, New York, N.Y.
World Trade Center

Steve Geller
World Trade Center

Howard G. Gelling, 28
World Trade Center

Peter Genco, 36, Rockville Centre, N.Y.
World Trade Center

Steven Genovese, 37, Basking Ridge, N.J.
World Trade Center

Alayne F. Gentul, 44, Mountain Lakes, N.J.
World Trade Center

Linda George, 27, Westboro, Mass.
American Flight 11 - WTC, airline passenger

Edward Geraghty
World Trade Center

Suzanne Geraty, 30, New York, N.Y.
World Trade Center

Ralph Gerhardt
World Trade Center

Robert J. Gerlich, 56, Monroe, Conn.
World Trade Center

Denis Germain
World Trade Center

Capt. Lawrence Daniel Getzfred, 57, Elgin, Neb.
Pentagon

James Gerard Geyer, 41, Rockville Centre, N.Y.
World Trade Center

Cortz Ghee, 54, Reisterstown, Md.
Pentagon

Lt. Vincent Giammona, 40, Valley Stream, N.Y.
World Trade Center

Debra L. Gibbon, 43, Hackettstown, N.J.
World Trade Center

James Giberson
World Trade Center

Brenda Gibson, 59, Falls Church, Va.
Pentagon

Craig Gibson, 37, New York, N.Y.
World Trade Center, South African

Ronnie Gies
World Trade Center

Andrew C. Gilbert, 39, Califon, N.J.
World Trade Center

Timothy P. Gilbert, 35, Lebanon, N.J.
World Trade Center

Paul G. Gilbey, 49, Chatham, N.J.
World Trade Center

Paul Gill
World Trade Center

Evan Gillette, 40
World Trade Center

Ron Gilligan, 43, East Norwalk, Conn.
World Trade Center

Lt. John Ginley
World Trade Center

Donna Giordano, 44, Sayreville, N.J.
World Trade Center

Jeffrey Giordano
World Trade Center

John Giordano, 47, Newburgh, N.Y.
World Trade Center

Jinny Lady Giraldo, 27
World Trade Center, Colombian

Kim Girolamo, 41
World Trade Center

Salvatore Gitto, 43, Manalapan, N.J.
World Trade Center

Keith Glascoe
World Trade Center

Thomas I. Glasser, 40, Summit, N.J.
World Trade Center

Edmund Glazer, 41, Los Angeles, Calif.
American Flight 11 - WTC, airline passenger

Harry Glenn, 38, Piscataway, N.J.
World Trade Center

Barry H. Glick, Wayne, N.J.
World Trade Center

Jeremy Glick, 31, West Milford, N.J.
United Flight 93 - Pennsylvania, airline passenger

Steven Lawrence Glick, 42, Greenwich, Conn.
World Trade Center

William (Bill) R. Godshalk, 35
World Trade Center

Michael Gogliornella, 43, New Providence, N.J.
World Trade Center

Brian Goldberg, 26, Union, N.J.
World Trade Center

Michelle Herman Goldstein, 31
World Trade Center

Steven Goldstein, 35, Princeton, N.J.
World Trade Center

Ron Golinski, 60, Columbia, Md.
Pentagon

Max Gomez
World Trade Center

Wilder Gomez
World Trade Center, Colombian

Ana Irene Medina Gonzalez
World Trade Center

Jenine Gonzalez, 28
World Trade Center

Joel Guevara Gonzalez
World Trade Center

Rosa J. Gonzalez, 32, Jersey City, N.J.
World Trade Center

Lynn Goodchild, 25, Attleboro, Mass.
United Flight 175 - WTC, airline passenger

Calvin J. Gooding, Riverside, N.Y.
World Trade Center

Lisa Fenn Gordenstein, 41, Needham, Mass.
American Flight 11 - WTC, airline passenger

Thomas Gorman, Middlesex, N.J.
World Trade Center

Kristin Gould
United Flight 93 - Pennsylvania, airline passenger

Douglas A. Gowell, 52, Methuen, Mass.
World Trade Center

Yuji Goya, 42
World Trade Center, Japanese

Christopher Grady, 39, Cranford, N.J.
World Trade Center

Edwin J. Graf, 48, Norwalk, Conn.
World Trade Center

David Graifman
World Trade Center

Lauren Grandcolas, 38, San Rafael, Calif.
United Flight 93 - Pennsylvania, airline passenger

Christopher S. Gray, 32, Weehawken, N.J.
World Trade Center

Ian Gray, 55, Washington, D.C.
American Flight 77 - Pentagon, airline passenger

James Gray
World Trade Center

John M. Grazioso, 41, Middletown, N.J.
World Trade Center

Tim Grazioso, 42, Clifton, N.J.
World Trade Center

Andrew Curry Green, 34, Los Angeles, Calif.
American Flight 11 - WTC, airline passenger

Wanda A. Green, 49, Linden, N.J.
United Flight 93 - Pennsylvania, flight crew

Donald F. Greene, 52, Greenwich, Conn.
United Flight 93 - Pennsylvania, airline passenger

Gayle R. Greene, 51, Montville, N.J.
World Trade Center

James Greenleaf, 32, Waterford, Conn.
World Trade Center

Eileen Greenstein, 52
World Trade Center

Lisa Gregg
World Trade Center

Denise Gregory
World Trade Center

Donald H. Gregory, 62, Ramsey, N.J.
World Trade Center

Florence Gregory, 38
World Trade Center

Pedro Grehan, 35, Hoboken, N.J.
World Trade Center

John Griffin, 38, Waldwick, N.J.
World Trade Center

Joan D. Griffith, Willingboro, N.J.
World Trade Center

Joseph F. Grillo, New York, N.Y.
World Trade Center

Francis Grogan, 76, Easton, Mass.
United Flight 175 - WTC, airline passenger

Linda Gronlund, 46, Warwick, N.Y.
United Flight 93 - Pennsylvania, airline passenger

Ken G. Grouzalis, Lyndhurst, N.J.
World Trade Center

Matthew J. Gryzmalski, New Hyde Park, N.Y.
World Trade Center

Joseph Grzelak
World Trade Center

Robert Joseph Gschaar, 55, Spring Valley, N.Y.
World Trade Center

Richard Guadagno, 38, Eureka, Calif.
United Flight 93 - Pennsylvania, airline passenger

Jose Guadalupe, 37
World Trade Center

Geoffrey E. Guja, 54, Lindenhurst, N.Y.
World Trade Center

Lt. Joseph Gullickson
World Trade Center

Philip T. Guza, 54, Sea Bright, N.J.
World Trade Center

Park Gye-hyong, 28
World Trade Center

Peter Gyulavary
World Trade Center

Gary Robert Haag, 36, Ossining, N.Y.
World Trade Center

Andrea Haberman, 25
World Trade Center

Paige Farley Hackel, 46, Newton, Mass.
American Flight 11 - WTC, airline passenger

Philip Haentzler, 49, New York, N.Y.
World Trade Center

Nizam Hafiz, 32
World Trade Center

Mary Lou Hague, 26, New York, N.Y.
World Trade Center

David Halderman, 40
World Trade Center

Diane M. Hale-McKinzy, 38, Alexandria, Va.
Pentagon

Richard Hall, 49
World Trade Center

Stanley Hall, 68, Rancho Palos Verdes, Calif.
American Flight 77 - Pentagon, airline passenger

Robert J. Halligan, 59, Basking Ridge, N.J.
World Trade Center

Lt. Vincent Halloran
World Trade Center

Carolyn Halmon, 49, Washington, D.C.
Pentagon

James D. Halvorson, 56, Greenwich, Conn.
World Trade Center

Felicia Hamilton, 62, Middletown, N.J.
World Trade Center

Robert Hamilton, 43, Washingtonville, N.Y.
World Trade Center

Carl Max Hammond, 37, Boston, Mass.
United Flight 175 - WTC, airline passenger

Frederic Kim Han, 45, Marlboro, N.J.
World Trade Center

Sean Hanley, 35
World Trade Center

Valerie Hanna, 57, Freeville, N.Y.
World Trade Center

Thomas Hannafin, 36, New York, N.Y.
World Trade Center

Kevin James Hannaford, 32, Basking Ridge, N.J.
World Trade Center

Michael L. Hannan, 34, Lynbrook, N.Y.
World Trade Center

Dana Hannon
World Trade Center

Christine Hanson, 2, Groton, Mass.
United Flight 175 - WTC, airline passenger

Peter Hanson, 32, Groton, Mass.
United Flight 175 - WTC, airline passenger

Vassilios G. Haramis
World Trade Center

James Haran, 41, Malverne, N.Y.
World Trade Center

Gerald F. Hardacre, 62, Carlsbad, Calif.
United Flight 175 - WTC, airline passenger

Timothy J. Hargrave, 38, N.J.
World Trade Center

Daniel Harlin
World Trade Center

Frances Haros, 76, New York, N.Y.
World Trade Center

Lt. Harvey Harrell
World Trade Center

Lt. Stephen Harrell
World Trade Center

Melissa Harrington Hughes, 31, San Francisco, Calif.
World Trade Center

Stewart Harris, 52, Marlboro, N.J.
World Trade Center

John Hart, 38, Danville, Calif.
World Trade Center

Eric Samadikan Hartono, 20, Boston, Mass.
Indonesian

John C. Hartz, 64, Basking Ridge, N.J.
World Trade Center

Emeric J. Harvey, 56, Montclair, N.J.
World Trade Center

Peter Hashem, 40, Tewksbury, Mass.
American Flight 11 - WTC, airline passenger

Capt. Thomas Haskell
World Trade Center

Timothy Haskell, 34, Seaford, N.Y.
World Trade Center

Leonard William Hatton, 45, Ridgefield Park, N.J.
World Trade Center

Capt. Terence S. Hatton, 41, New York, N.Y.
World Trade Center

Michael Haub
World Trade Center

Tim Haviland, 41, Oceanside, N.Y.
World Trade Center

Donald G. Havlish, 53, Yardley, Pa.
World Trade Center

James E. Hayden, 47, Westford, Mass.
United Flight 175 - WTC, airline passenger

Robert Hayes, 37, Amesbury, Mass.
American Flight 11 - WTC, airline passenger

W. Ward Haynes, 35, Rye, N.Y.
World Trade Center

Lt. Michael Healey
World Trade Center

Roberta Bernstein Heber, 60, New York, N.Y.
World Trade Center

Charles Heeran
World Trade Center

John Heffernan, 37
World Trade Center

Michele Heidenberger, 57, Chevy Chase, Md.
American Flight 77 - Pentagon, flight crew

Sheila Hein, 51, University Park, Md.
Pentagon

Joseph H. Heller, 37, Ridgefield, Conn.
World Trade Center

JoAnn Heltibridle, 46, Springfield, N.J.
World Trade Center

Ronald John Hemenway, 37, Shawnee, Kan.
Pentagon

Mark F. Hemschoot, 45, Red Bank, N.J.
World Trade Center

Ronnie Henderson
World Trade Center

Brian Hennessey, 35, Ringoes, N.J.
World Trade Center

Ted Hennessy, 35, Belmont, Mass.
American Flight 11 - WTC, airline passenger

Joseph Henry
World Trade Center

William Henry, 49
World Trade Center

John Henwood
World Trade Center

Robert Hepburn, 39, Union, N.J.
World Trade Center

Molly Herencia, 47
World Trade Center

Lindsay Coates Herkness, 58, New York, N.Y.
World Trade Center

Norberto Hernandez, 42, New York, N.Y.
World Trade Center

Gary Herold, 44
World Trade Center

Thomas Hetzel, 33
World Trade Center

Capt. Brian Hickey
World Trade Center

Lt. Timothy Higgins, 43
World Trade Center

Robert Higley, 29, New Fairfield, Conn.
World Trade Center

Neal Hinds, 28
World Trade Center

Mark D. Hindy, 28, New York, N.Y.
World Trade Center

Heather Ho, 32, New York, N.Y.
World Trade Center

Tara Hobbs, 31
World Trade Center

Tom Hobbs
World Trade Center

James Hobin, 47, Marlborough, Conn.
World Trade Center

Robert Wayne Hobson, 36, New Providence, N.J.
World Trade Center

Patrick Aloysius Hoey, 53, Middletown, N.J.
World Trade Center

John Hofer, 45, Bellflower, Calif.
American Flight 11 - WTC, airline passenger

Frederick J. Hoffman, 53, N.J.
World Trade Center

Joseph Hoffman, 43
World Trade Center

Marcia Hoffman
World Trade Center

Michele L. Hoffman, 27, N.J.
World Trade Center

Stephen G. Hoffman
World Trade Center

Judith Florence Hofmiller, 53, Brookfield, Conn.
World Trade Center

Maj. Wallace Cole Hogan, 40, Fla.
Pentagon

Thomas Warren Hohlweck, 56, Harrison, N.Y.
World Trade Center

Jonathan Hohmann, 48, Annadale, N.Y.
World Trade Center

Cora Holland, 52, Sudbury, Mass.
American Flight 11 - WTC, airline passenger

John Holland, 30
World Trade Center

Joseph Francis Holland, 32, Glen Rock, N.J.
World Trade Center

Jimmie Ira Holley, 54, Lanham, Md.
Pentagon

Elizabeth Holmes, 42, New York, N.Y.
World Trade Center

Thomas P. Holohan, 36, Chester, N.Y.
World Trade Center

Herbert Homer, 48, Milford, Mass.
United Flight 175 - WTC, airline passenger

LeRoy Homer, 36, Marlton, N.J.
United Flight 93 - Pennsylvania, flight crew

Brad Hoorn, 22
World Trade Center

Montgomery Hord, Pelham, N.Y.
World Trade Center

Michael Horn
World Trade Center

Matthew D. Horning, 26, Scotch Plains, N.J.
World Trade Center

Robert Horohoe, 31, New York, N.Y.
World Trade Center

Michael R. Horrocks, 38, Glen Mills, Pa.
United Flight 175 - WTC, flight crew

Aaron Horwitz
World Trade Center

Malverse Houscal, N.J.
World Trade Center

Charles J. Houston
World Trade Center

Uhuru Houston, 32
World Trade Center

Angela Houtz, 27, La Plata, Md.
Pentagon

George Howard, 45, Hicksville, N.Y.
World Trade Center

Brady Howell, 26, Arlington, Va.
Pentagon

Michael Howell
World Trade Center

Jennifer Howley, 34, New Hyde Park, N.Y.
World Trade Center

Milagros Hromada
World Trade Center

Steve Huczko, Bethlehem, N.J.
World Trade Center

Kris R. Hughes
World Trade Center

Paul Hughes, 38, Stamford, Conn.
World Trade Center

Thomas Hughes, 46
World Trade Center

Timothy Robert Hughes, 43, Madison, N.J.
World Trade Center

Susan Huie, 43, Fair Lawn, N.J.
World Trade Center

Nicholas Humber, 60, Newton, Mass.
American Flight 11 - WTC, airline passenger

(Casey) Kathleen Hunt
World Trade Center

William C. Hunt, 32, Norwalk, Conn.
World Trade Center

Joseph Hunter, 32
World Trade Center

Peggie Hurt, 36, Crewe, Va.
Pentagon

Robert Hussa, 51, Roslyn, N.Y.
World Trade Center

Lt. Col. Stephen Neil Hyland, 45, Burke, Va.
Pentagon

Robert J. Hymel, Woodbridge, Va.
Pentagon

Capt. Walter Hynes, 46, Belle Harbor, N.Y.
World Trade Center

Lee Hyun-joon, 34
World Trade Center

Zuhtu Ibis, 25, Clifton, N.J.
World Trade Center

Jonathan Ielpi
World Trade Center

Michael Patrick Iken, 37, New York, N.Y.
World Trade Center

Capt. Frederick Ill
World Trade Center

Anthony P. Infante, 47, Chatham, N.J.
World Trade Center

Louis Inghilterra
World Trade Center

Christopher N. Ingrassia, 28, Watchung, N.J.
World Trade Center

Paul Innella, 33, East Brunswick, N.J.
World Trade Center

Doug Irgang
World Trade Center

William Iselepis, 33
World Trade Center

Taizo Ishikawa, 50
World Trade Center, Japanese

Aram Iskenderian, 41, Merrick, N.Y.
World Trade Center

John Iskyan, 41, Wilton, Conn.
World Trade Center

Kazushige Ito, 35
World Trade Center, Japanese

Sgt. Maj. Lacey B. Ivory, 43, Woodbridge, Va.
Pentagon

Virginia Jablonski, 49, Matawan, N.J.
World Trade Center

Bryan Jack, 48, Alexandria, Va.
American Flight 77 - Pentagon, airline passenger

Brooke Jackman, 23, New York, N.Y.
World Trade Center

Aaron Jacobs, 27
World Trade Center

Jason K. Jacobs, 32, Randolph, N.J.
World Trade Center

Michael Grady Jacobs, 54, Danbury, Conn.
World Trade Center

Steven Jacobson, 53, New York, N.Y.
World Trade Center

Steven D. Jacoby, 43, Alexandria, Va.
American Flight 77 - Pentagon, airline passenger

Robert Jalbert, 61, Swampscott, Mass.
United Flight 175 - WTC, airline passenger

Amy Jarret, 28, North Smithfield, R.I.
United Flight 175 - WTC, flight crew

Paul Jeffers, 39, New York, N.Y.
World Trade Center

John Jenkins, 45, Cambridge, Mass.
American Flight 11 - WTC, airline passenger

Alan K. Jensen, 49, Wyckoff, N.J.
World Trade Center

Prem N. Jerath, Edison, N.J.
World Trade Center

Hweidar Jian, 42, East Brunswick, N.J.
World Trade Center

Lt. Col. Dennis M. Johnson, 48, Wis.
Pentagon

Scott Johnson, 26
World Trade Center

William Johnston, 31
World Trade Center

Allison Horstmann Jones, 31, Bernardsville, N.J.
World Trade Center

Arthur J. Jones, Ossining, N.Y.
World Trade Center

Charles Jones, 48, Bedford, Mass.
American Flight 11 - WTC, airline passenger

Donald W. Jones, 43, Fairless Hills, Pa.
World Trade Center

Judith Jones, 53, Woodbridge, Va.
Pentagon

Linda Jones, 50
World Trade Center

Mary S. Jones, New York, N.Y.
World Trade Center

Lee Jong-min
World Trade Center

Andrew Jordan
World Trade Center

Robert T. Jordan, 34, Williston, N.Y.
World Trade Center

Karl Joseph
World Trade Center

Stephen Joseph, 39, Franklin Park, N.J.
World Trade Center

Lt. Anthony Jovic
World Trade Center

Angel Juarbe
World Trade Center

Ann Judge, 49, Great Falls, Va.
American Flight 77 - Pentagon, airline passenger

The Rev. Mychal Judge, 68, New York, N.Y.
World Trade Center

Paul Jurgens, Levittown, N.Y.
World Trade Center

Shari Kandell, 27, Wyckoff, N.J.
World Trade Center

Howard L. Kane, 36, Hazlet, N.J.
World Trade Center

Jennifer L. Kane, 26, Fair Lawn, N.J.
World Trade Center

Vincent Kane
World Trade Center

Joon Kang, 34, Riverdale, N.J.
World Trade Center

Sheldon R. Kanter, 53, Edison, N.J.
World Trade Center

Deborah H. Kaplan, 45, Paramus, N.J.
World Trade Center

Robin Kaplan, 33, Westboro, Mass.
American Flight 11 - WTC, airline passenger

Alvin P. Kappelman, 57, Green Brook, N.J.
World Trade Center

Charles Karczewski, 34, Union, N.J.
World Trade Center

Douglas G. Karpiloff, Mamaroneck, N.Y.
World Trade Center

Charles L. Kasper
World Trade Center

Andrew Kates, 37, New York, N.Y.
World Trade Center

Sgt. Robert Kaulfers, 49, Kenilworth, N.J.
World Trade Center

Don J. Kauth, 51, Saratoga Springs, N.Y.
World Trade Center

Hideya Kawauchi, 36
World Trade Center, Japanese

Edward T. Keane, 66, West Caldwell, N.J.
World Trade Center

Richard Keane, 54, Wethersfield, Conn.
World Trade Center

Karol Keasler
World Trade Center

Barbara Keating, 72, Palm Springs, Calif.
American Flight 11 - WTC, airline passenger

Paul Keating
World Trade Center

Leo R. Keene, 33, Westfield, N.J.
World Trade Center

L. Russell Keene III
World Trade Center

Brenda Kegler, 49, Washington, D.C.
Pentagon

Chandler Keller, 29, El Segundo, Calif.
American Flight 77 - Pentagon, airline passenger

Joseph J. Keller, 31, Park Ridge, N.J.
World Trade Center

Peter Rodney Kellerman, 35, New York, N.Y.
World Trade Center

Joseph P. Kellett
World Trade Center

Frederick Kelley, Huntington, N.Y.
World Trade Center

James Joseph Kelly, 39, Oceanside, N.Y.
World Trade Center

Richard J. Kelly, 50, Graniteville, N.Y.
World Trade Center

Thomas R. Kelly
World Trade Center

Thomas W. Kelly, 51, New York, N.Y.
World Trade Center

Timothy Kelly
World Trade Center

William H. Kelly, 24, Brant Beach, N.J.
World Trade Center

Robert C. Kennedy, 55, Toms River, N.J.
World Trade Center

Susan Schular Kennedy
World Trade Center

Thomas Kennedy
World Trade Center

Yvonne Kennedy
American Flight 77 - Pentagon, airline passenger

John Keohane, 41, Jersey City, N.J.
World Trade Center

Ralph Kershaw, 52, Manchester-by-the-Sea, Mass.
United Flight 175 - WTC, airline passenger

Lt. Ronald Kerwin
World Trade Center

Howard L. Kestembaum, 56, Upper Montclair, N.J.
World Trade Center

Norma Khan, 45, Reston, Va.
American Flight 77 - Pentagon, airline passenger

Taimour Khan
World Trade Center

Seilai Khoo
World Trade Center

Michael Kiefer
World Trade Center

Andrew Kim
World Trade Center

Don Kim, 34
World Trade Center

Mary Kimelman, 34
World Trade Center

Sue Kim-Hanson, 35, Groton, Mass.
United Flight 175 - WTC, airline passenger

Heinrich Kimmig, 43
United Flight 175 - WTC, airline passenger

Karen A. Kincaid, 40
American Flight 77 - Pentagon, airline passenger

Amy King, 29, Stafford Springs, Conn.
United Flight 175 - WTC, flight crew

Andrew Marshall King, 42, Princeton, N.J.
World Trade Center

Lucille King, 59
World Trade Center

Robert King
World Trade Center

Lisa M. King-Johnson
World Trade Center

Brian Kinney, 29, Lowell, Mass.
United Flight 175 - WTC, airline passenger

Takashi Kinoshita, 46
World Trade Center, Japanese

Glenn Kirwin, 40, Scarsdale, N.Y.
World Trade Center

Alan D. Kleinberg, 39, East Brunswick, N.J.
World Trade Center

Karen Klitzman
World Trade Center

Andrew Knox, 30
World Trade Center

Thomas P. Knox, 31, Hoboken, N.J.
World Trade Center

Gary Koecheler, 57, Harrison, N.Y.
World Trade Center

Ryan Kohart, 26, Garden City, N.Y.
World Trade Center

Vanessa L. Kolpak
World Trade Center

Bon-seok Koo, 32, River Edge, N.J.
World Trade Center

Scott Kopytko
World Trade Center

Bojan Kostic
World Trade Center

Danielle Kousoulis, 29, N.J.
World Trade Center

David Kovalcin, 42, Hudson, N.H.
American Flight 11 - WTC, airline passenger

William Krukowski
World Trade Center

Toshiya Kuge, 20, Tokyo, Japan
United Flight 93 - Pennsylvania, airline passenger

Kenneth Kumpel
World Trade Center

Frederick Kuo
World Trade Center

Thomas Kuveikis
World Trade Center

Victor Kwarkye, 35
World Trade Center

Angela R. Kyte, 49, Boonton, N.J.
World Trade Center

Kathryn LaBorie, 44, Providence, R.I.
United Flight 175 - WTC, flight crew

Andrew LaCorte, 61, Jersey City, N.J.
World Trade Center

James P. Ladley, 41, Colts Neck, N.J.
World Trade Center

David Laforge
World Trade Center

Michael Laforte, 39, Holmdel, N.J.
World Trade Center

Neil K. Lai, 59, East Windsor, N.J.
World Trade Center

Vincent A. Laieta, 31, Edison, N.J.
World Trade Center

William Lake
World Trade Center

Frank Lalama, 45, Nutley, N.J.
World Trade Center

Chow K. Lam, 48, Maywood, N.J.
World Trade Center

Lt. Michael Scott Lamana, 31, Baton Rouge, La.
Pentagon

Steven LaMantia, 38, Darien, Conn.
World Trade Center

Robert Lane
World Trade Center

Brendan Lang, 30, Red Bank, N.J.
World Trade Center

Rosanne Lang, 42, Middletown, N.J.
World Trade Center

Venessa Langer, 29
World Trade Center

Mary Lou Langley, 53
World Trade Center

Peter Langone, 41, Roslyn Heights, N.Y.
World Trade Center

Thomas Langone, 39
World Trade Center

Ruth S. Lapin, 53, East Windsor, N.J.
World Trade Center

Robin Larkey
World Trade Center

Judy Larocque, 50, Framingham, Mass.
American Flight 11 - WTC, airline passenger

Christopher Larrabee, 26, Palos Verdes Estates, Calif.
World Trade Center

Scott Larsen
World Trade Center

John Larson, 37, Colonia, N.J.
World Trade Center

N. Janis Lasden, 46, Peabody, Mass.
American Flight 11 - WTC, airline passenger

Nicholas C. Lassman
World Trade Center

Paul Laszczynski, Wayne, N.J.
World Trade Center

Jeffrey Latouche, 49
World Trade Center

Jeannine LaVerde, 36, Meiers Corner, N.Y.
World Trade Center

Anna Laverty, 52, Middletown, N.J.
World Trade Center

Bob Lawrence
World Trade Center

David W. Laychak, 40, Manassas, Va.
Pentagon

Eugene Lazar, 27, New York, N.Y.
World Trade Center

Lt. Joseph Leavey
World Trade Center

Neil Leavy, 34, New York, N.Y.
World Trade Center

Robert LeBlanc, 70, Lee, N.H.
United Flight 175 - WTC, airline passenger

Alan Lederman, 43
World Trade Center

Daniel John Lee, 34, Los Angeles, Calif.
American Flight 11 - WTC, airline passenger

Dong Lee, 48, Leesburg, Va.
American Flight 77 - Pentagon, airline passenger

Juanita Lee, 44
World Trade Center

Kathryn Lee, 55, N.Y.
World Trade Center

Lorraine Lee
World Trade Center

Myoung W. Lee, 41, Lyndhurst, N.J.
World Trade Center

Richard Y.C. Lee, 34, Great Neck, N.Y.
World Trade Center

Stuart Lee, 31
World Trade Center

Adriana Legro, 32, Elmhurst, N.Y.
World Trade Center, Colombian

Edward Lehman, 42
World Trade Center

David R. Leistman, 43, Garden City, N.Y.
World Trade Center

David LeMagne, North Bergen, N.J.
World Trade Center

Joseph A. Lenihan, 41, Greenwich, Conn.
World Trade Center

John J. Lennon, 44, Howell, N.J.
World Trade Center

John Robinson Lenoir, 38, Locust Valley, N.Y.
World Trade Center

Jorge Leon
World Trade Center

Matthew G. Leonard, 38, New York, N.Y.
World Trade Center

Michael Lepore, 39, New York, N.Y.
World Trade Center

Jeffrey Earle LeVeen, 55, Manhasset, N.Y.
World Trade Center

John Levi, New York, N.Y.
World Trade Center

Neil D. Levin, 47
World Trade Center

Daniel C. Lewin, 31, Brookline, Mass.
American Flight 11 - WTC, airline passenger

Adam J. Lewis
World Trade Center

Jennifer Lewis, 38, Culpeper, Va.
American Flight 77 - Pentagon, flight crew

Kenneth Lewis, 49, Culpeper, Va.
American Flight 77 - Pentagon, flight crew

Margaret S. Lewis, 49, Elizabeth, N.J.
World Trade Center

Daniel Libretti
World Trade Center

Samantha Lightbourn-Allen, 36, Hillside, Md.
Pentagon

Steven B. Lillianthal, 38, Millburn, N.J.
World Trade Center

Carlos Lillo, 37, Babylon, N.Y.
World Trade Center

Craig Lilore, 30, Lyndhurst, N.J.
World Trade Center

Thomas V. Linehan, 39, Montville, N.J.
World Trade Center

Robert Linnane
World Trade Center

Alansan Linton
World Trade Center

Diane T. Lipari, 32
World Trade Center

Kenneth P. Lira, 28, Paterson, N.J.
World Trade Center

Ming-Hao Liu, Livingston, N.J.
World Trade Center

Joseph Livera, 67
World Trade Center

Nancy Liz, 39
World Trade Center

Harold Lizcano
World Trade Center

Martin Lizzul, 31, Dix Hills, N.Y.
World Trade Center

George Llanes
World Trade Center

Elizabeth Claire Logler, 31, New York, N.Y.
World Trade Center

Catherine Loguidice, 30, New York, N.Y.
World Trade Center

Michael Lomax
World Trade Center

Maj. Steve Long, 39, Ga.
Pentagon

Laura M. Longing, 35, Pearl River, N.Y.
World Trade Center

Salvatore Lopes
World Trade Center

Daniel Lopez
World Trade Center

Maclovio Lopez, 41, Norwalk, Calif.
United Flight 175 - WTC, airline passenger

Stuart Louis
World Trade Center

Joseph Lovero, 60, Jersey City, N.J.
World Trade Center

Sara Low, 28, Batesville, Ark.
American Flight 11 - WTC, flight crew

Garry Lozier, 47, Darien, Conn.
World Trade Center

Edward (Ted) H. Luckett, 40, Fair Haven, N.J.
World Trade Center

Mark G. Ludvigsen
World Trade Center

Sean T. Lugano
World Trade Center

Marie Lukas
World Trade Center

Gary Lutnick
World Trade Center

Linda Luzzicone, 33, New York, N.Y.
World Trade Center

CeeCee Lyles, Fort Myers, Fla.
United Flight 93 - Pennsylvania, flight crew

Farrell Peter Lynch, 39, Centerport, N.Y.
World Trade Center

James Lynch, Manassas, Va.
Pentagon

James Lynch, Woodbridge, N.J.
World Trade Center

Michael Lynch, 30
World Trade Center

Richard Dennis Lynch, 30
World Trade Center

Robert H. Lynch, 44, Cranford, N.J.
World Trade Center

Sean Lynch, Lynnfield, Mass.
World Trade Center

Sean P. Lynch, 37, Morristown, N.J.
World Trade Center

Terrance M. Lynch, 49, Alexandria, Va.
Pentagon

Michael Lyons, 33, Hawthorne, N.Y.
World Trade Center

Nehamon Lyons, 30, Mobile, Ala.
Pentagon

Patrick Lyons
World Trade Center

Robert Mace
World Trade Center

Marianne MacFarlane, 34, Revere, Mass.
United Flight 175 - WTC, airline passenger

Jan Maciejewski, New York, N.Y.
World Trade Center

Susan MacKay, 44, Westford, Mass.
American Flight 11 - WTC, airline passenger

Catherine MacRea
World Trade Center

Richard B. Madden, 35, Westfield, N.J.
World Trade Center

Dennis A. Madsen, 53, Glen Gardner, N.J.
World Trade Center

Noell Maerz, 29, Long Island, N.Y.
World Trade Center

Joseph Maffeo
World Trade Center

Joseph Maggitti, 47, Abingdon, Md.
World Trade Center

Ronald E. Magnuson, 57, Park Ridge, N.J.
World Trade Center

Thomas Mahon, 37, East Norwich, N.Y.
World Trade Center

William Mahoney
World Trade Center

Joseph Maio, 32, Roslyn, N.Y.
World Trade Center

Takashi Makmoto, 49
World Trade Center, Japanese

Myrna Maldonado, 49, New York, N.Y.
World Trade Center

Alfred R. Maler, 39, Morris Township, N.J.
World Trade Center

Gregory J. Malone
World Trade Center

Edward Francis (Teddy) Maloney, 32, Norwalk, CT
World Trade Center

Joseph Maloney, 46, Farmingville, N.Y.
World Trade Center

Christian Maltby, 37, Chatham, N.J.
World Trade Center

Joseph Mangano, 53, Jackson, N.J.
World Trade Center

Sara Manley, 31, New York, N.Y.
World Trade Center

Debra M. Mannetta, 31, Islip, N.Y.
World Trade Center

Alfred Marchand, 44, Alamogordo, N.M.
United Flight 175 - WTC, flight crew

Joseph Marchbanks
World Trade Center

Hilda Marcin, 79, Budd Lake, N.J.
United Flight 93 - Pennsylvania, airline passenger

Edward J. Mardovich, Lloyd Harbor, N.Y.
World Trade Center

Lt. Charles Margiotta
World Trade Center

Louis Neil Mariani, 59, Derry, N.H.
United Flight 175 - WTC, airline passenger

Kenneth Marino
World Trade Center

Lester Vincent Marino, 57, Massapequa, N.Y.
World Trade Center

Vita Marino
World Trade Center

Kevin Marlo, 28, New York, N.Y.
World Trade Center

Jose J. Marrero, 32, Old Bridge, N.J.
World Trade Center

John Marshall
World Trade Center

Shelley A. Marshall, 37, Marbury, Md.
Pentagon

James Martello, 41, Rumson, N.J.
World Trade Center

Michael A. Marti, 26, Glendale, N.Y.
World Trade Center

Karen Martin, 40, Danvers, Mass.
American Flight 11 - WTC, flight crew

Lt. Peter Martin
World Trade Center

Teresa Martin, 45, Stafford, Va.
Pentagon

William Martin, 35, Denville, N.J.
World Trade Center

Brian E. Martineau, 37, Edison, N.J.
World Trade Center

Edward J. Martinez, 60, New York, N.Y.
World Trade Center

Waleska Martinez, 38, Jersey City, N.J.
United Flight 93 - Pennsylvania, airline passenger

Lizie Martinez-Calderon, 32
World Trade Center

Lt. Paul Martini
World Trade Center

Joseph Mascali
World Trade Center

Ada L. Mason, 50, Springfield, Va.
Pentagon

Nick (Nicholas) Massa, 65
World Trade Center

Michael Massaroli, 38, New York, N.Y.
World Trade Center

Philip W. Mastandrea, 42, Chatham, N.J.
World Trade Center

Philip W. Mastrandrea, 42, Chatham, N.J.
World Trade Center

Rudy Mastrocinque, 43, Kings Park, N.Y.
World Trade Center

Joseph Mathai, 49, Arlington, Mass.
World Trade Center

Charles M. Mathers, 61, Sea Girt, N.J.
World Trade Center

William A. Mathesen
World Trade Center

William A. Matheson, 40, Morris Township, N.J.
World Trade Center

Margaret Mattic, 51
World Trade Center

Marcello Mattricciano
World Trade Center

Lt. Col. Dean E. Mattson, 57, Calif.
Pentagon

Robert D. Mattson, 54, Rockaway, N.J.
World Trade Center

Walter Matuza, 39, New York, N.Y.
World Trade Center

Lt. Gen. Timothy Maude, 53, Fort Myer, Va.
Pentagon

Charles J. Mauro, 38, N.J.
World Trade Center

Charles J. (Chuck) Mauro, 65, Eltingville, N.Y.
World Trade Center

Nancy T. Mauro, 51, Forest Hills, N.Y.
World Trade Center

Robert J. Maxwell, 53, Manassas, Va.
Pentagon

Renee May, 39, Baltimore, Md.
American Flight 77 - Pentagon, flight crew

Tyrone May, 44, Rahway, N.J.
World Trade Center

Keithroy Maynard
World Trade Center

Robert J. Mayo, 46, Morganville, N.J.
World Trade Center

Kathy Mazza, Farmingdale, N.Y.
World Trade Center

Edward Mazzella, 62, Monroe, N.Y.
World Trade Center

Kaaria Mbaya, 39, Edison, N.J.
World Trade Center

James J. McAlary, 42, Spring Lake Heights, N.J.
World Trade Center

Brian McAleese
World Trade Center

Colin Richard McArthur, 52, Howell, N.J.
World Trade Center

John McAvoy, 47, New York, N.Y.
World Trade Center

Ken McBrayer
World Trade Center

Brendan McCabe, 40, Sayville, N.Y.
World Trade Center

Michael McCabe, 42, Rumson, N.J.
World Trade Center

Thomas McCann
World Trade Center

Kevin McCarthy, 42, Fairfield, Conn.
World Trade Center

Michael Desmond McCarthy, 33, Huntington, N.Y.
World Trade Center

Robert Garvin McCarthy, 33, Stony Point, N.Y.
World Trade Center

Katie McCloskey, 25
World Trade Center

Juliana Valentine McCourt, 4, New London, Conn.
United Flight 175 - WTC, airline passenger

Ruth McCourt, 45, New London, Conn.
United Flight 175 - WTC, airline passenger

Tonyell McDay, 25, Colonia, N.J.
World Trade Center

Matthew T. McDermott, 34, Basking Ridge, N.J.
World Trade Center

Joseph McDonald, 43, Livingston, N.J.
World Trade Center

Michael McDonnell, 34, Red Bank, N.J.
World Trade Center

John F. McDowell, 33, New York, N.Y.
World Trade Center

Eamon McEneaney, 46, New Canaan, Conn.
World Trade Center

Katherine (Katie) McGarry-Noack, 30, Hoboken, N.J.
World Trade Center

Daniel F. McGinley, 40, Ridgewood, N.J.
World Trade Center

Mark McGinly, Vienna, Va.
World Trade Center

Lt. William E. McGinn, 43, New York, N.Y.
World Trade Center

Thomas H. McGinnis, 41, Oakland, N.J.
World Trade Center

Michael G. McGinty, 42, Foxboro, Mass.
World Trade Center

Ann McGovern
World Trade Center

Scott M. McGovern, 35, Wyckoff, N.J.
World Trade Center

William J. McGovern, 49, Smithtown, N.Y.
World Trade Center

Stacey McGowan
World Trade Center

Francis Noel McGuinn, 50, Rye, N.Y.
World Trade Center

Thomas McGuinness, 42, Portsmouth, N.H.
American Flight 11 - WTC, flight crew

Patrick J. McGuire, 40, Madison, N.J.
World Trade Center

Thomas McHale, 33, Huntington, N.Y.
World Trade Center

Keith McHeffey, 31, Monmouth Beach, N.J.
World Trade Center

Ann M. McHugh
World Trade Center

Dennis P. McHugh
World Trade Center

Michael Edward McHugh, 35, Tuckahoe, N.Y.
World Trade Center

Robert G. McIlvaine, 26, New York, N.Y.
World Trade Center

Donald McIntyre, New City, N.Y.
World Trade Center

Stephanie McKenna, 45, New York, N.Y.
World Trade Center

Molly McKenzie, 38, Dale City, Va.
Pentagon

Barry McKeon, Yorktown Heights, N.Y.
World Trade Center

George P. McLaughlin, 36, Hoboken, N.J.
World Trade Center

Robert C. McLaughlin, 29
World Trade Center

Robert Mcmahon
World Trade Center

Edmund M. McNally, 40, Fair Haven, N.J.
World Trade Center

Daniel McNeal, 29
World Trade Center

Walter McNeil, E. Stroudsburg, Pa.
World Trade Center

Sean McNulty, 30
World Trade Center

Robert McPadden
World Trade Center

Terence McShane
World Trade Center

Timothy McSweeney
World Trade Center

Martin McWilliams, 35
World Trade Center

Damian Meehan, 32, Glen Rock, N.J.
World Trade Center

William Meehan, 49, Darien, Conn.
World Trade Center

Raymond Meisenheimer
World Trade Center

Antonio Melendez
World Trade Center

Christopher D. Mello, 25, Boston, Mass.
American Flight 11 - WTC, airline passenger

Stuart Todd Meltzer, 32, Syosett, N.Y.
World Trade Center

Dora Menchaca, 45, Santa Monica, Calif.
American Flight 77 - Pentagon, airline passenger

Charles Mendez
World Trade Center

Lizette Mendoza, 33
World Trade Center

Wolfgang Menzel, 60
United Flight 175 - WTC, airline passenger

Steve Mercado, 38, New York, N.Y.
World Trade Center

Ralph Mercurio, 47, Rockville Centre, N.Y.
World Trade Center

Alan H. Merdinger, 47, South Whitehall Township, Pa.
World Trade Center

Yamel Merino, 24, Yonkers, N.Y.
World Trade Center

George Merkouris, Levittown, N.Y.
World Trade Center

Raymond J. Metz, 37, Trumbull, Conn.
World Trade Center

Jill Metzler, 32
World Trade Center

David R. Meyer, 57, Glen Rock, N.J.
World Trade Center

William E. Micciulli, 30, Old Bridge, N.J.
World Trade Center

Martin P. Michaelstein, 57, Morristown, N.J.
World Trade Center

Patricia E. (Patti) Mickley, 41, Springfield, Va.
Pentagon

Maj. Ronald D. Milam, 33, Washington, DC
Pentagon

Peter T. Milano, 43, Middletown, N.J.
World Trade Center

Gregory Milanowycz, 25, Cranford, N.J.
World Trade Center

Sharon Cristina Millan Paz, 30
World Trade Center, Colombian

Douglas C. Miller, 34, Port Jervis, N.Y.
World Trade Center

Henry Miller
World Trade Center

Michael Miller, 39, Milford, Conn.
World Trade Center

Nicole Miller, 21, San Jose, Calif.
United Flight 93 - Pennsylvania, airline passenger

Robert Miller, 55
World Trade Center

Robert A. Miller, 46, Old Bridge, N.J.
World Trade Center

Robert Minara
World Trade Center

William Minardi, 46, Bedford, N.Y.
World Trade Center

Louis Minervino, 54, Middletown, N.J.
World Trade Center

Thomas Mingione
World Trade Center

Wilbert Miraille, 29, New York, N.Y.
World Trade Center

Domenick Mircovich, 40, Closter, N.J.
World Trade Center

Rajesh A. Mirpuri, 30, Englewood, N.J.
World Trade Center

Lt. Paul Mitchell
World Trade Center

Jeff Mladenik, 43, Hinsdale, Ill.
American Flight 11 - WTC, airline passenger

Frank V. Moccia
World Trade Center

Capt. Louis Modafferi
World Trade Center

Mubarak Mohammad, 23, East Orange, N.J.
World Trade Center

Boyie Mohammed
World Trade Center

Lt. Dennis Mojica, 50, New York, N.Y.
World Trade Center

Manuel Mojica, 37, Bellmore, N.Y.
World Trade Center

Carl Molinaro
World Trade Center

Justin J. Molisani, 42, Middletown Township, N.J.
World Trade Center

Brian Patrick Monaghan, 21, New York, N.Y.
World Trade Center

John G. Monahan, 47, Ocean Township, N.J.
World Trade Center

Craig D. Montano, 38, Glen Ridge, N.J.
World Trade Center

Michael Montesi, 39, Highland Mills, N.Y.
World Trade Center

Antonio Montoya, 46, East Boston, Mass.
American Flight 11 - WTC, airline passenger

Carlos Montoya
American Flight 11 - WTC, airline passenger,
Colombian

Cheryl Monyak, 43, Greenwich, Conn.
World Trade Center

Capt. Thomas Moody
World Trade Center

Sharon Moore
World Trade Center

Laura Lee Morabito, 34, Framingham, Mass.
American Flight 11 - WTC, airline passenger

Martin Morales
World Trade Center

Paula Morales, 42
World Trade Center

Jerry Moran, 39, Upper Marlboro, Md.
Pentagon

John Moran
World Trade Center

Lindsay S. Morehouse, 24, Branford, Conn.
World Trade Center

George Morell, 47, Mt. Kisco, N.Y.
World Trade Center

Steven Morello, 52, Bayonne, N.J.
World Trade Center

Vincent Morello
World Trade Center

Arturo Alva Moreno
World Trade Center

Roy Wallace Moreno, 42
World Trade Center

Yvette Moreno
World Trade Center

Richard Morgan, 63
World Trade Center

Dennis G. Moroney
World Trade Center

John Morris, 46, N.J.
World Trade Center

Odessa V. Morris, 54, Upper Marlboro, Md.
Pentagon

Seth Morris
World Trade Center

Jorge Luis Morron Garcia, 39
World Trade Center, Colombian

Fred V. Morrone, 63, Lakewood, N.J.
World Trade Center

William Moskal, 50, Brecksville, Ohio
World Trade Center

Brian Anthony Moss, 34, Sperry, Okla.
Pentagon

Mark Motroni, 56, North Bergen, N.J.
World Trade Center

Jude Moussa
World Trade Center

Peter C. Moutos, 44, Chatham, N.J.
World Trade Center

Ted Moy, 48, Silver Spring, Md.
Pentagon

Christopher Mozzillo
World Trade Center

Stephen V. Mulderry, New York, N.Y.
World Trade Center

Richard Muldowney
World Trade Center

Michael Mullan
World Trade Center

Dennis Mulligan
World Trade Center

James Donald Munhall, 45, Ridgewood, N.J.
World Trade Center

Carlos Mario Munoz, 43
World Trade Center, Colombian

Theresa Munson, 54
World Trade Center

Robert Murach, 45, Montclair, N.J.
World Trade Center

Cesar Augusto Murillo, 31, Norwalk, Conn.
World Trade Center, Colombian

Marc A. Murolo, Hoboken, N.J.
World Trade Center

Brian Murphy
World Trade Center

Charles Murphy, Ridgewood, N.J.
World Trade Center

Christopher W. Murphy, 35, Stamford, Conn.
World Trade Center

Edward C. Murphy, 42, Clifton, N.J.
World Trade Center

James F. Murphy, 30, Garden City, N.Y.
World Trade Center

James Thomas Murphy, 35, Middletown, N.J.
World Trade Center

Kevin James Murphy, 40, Northport, N.Y.
World Trade Center

Lt. Cmdr. Patrick Jude Murphy, 38, Flossmoor, Ill.
Pentagon

Patrick S. Murphy, 36, Millburn, N.J.
World Trade Center

Lt. Raymond Murphy, 50
World Trade Center

Susan D. Murrary, 54, New Providence, N.J.
World Trade Center

John J. Murray, 32, Hoboken, N.J.
World Trade Center

Louis J. Nacke, 42, New Hope, Pa.
United Flight 93 - Pennsylvania, airline passenger

Lt. Robert Nagel
World Trade Center

Mildred Naiman, Andover, Mass.
American Flight 11 - WTC, airline passenger

Alexander J. Napier, 38, Morris Township, N.J.
World Trade Center

John Napolitano, 33, Ronkonkoma, N.Y.
World Trade Center

Catherine Nardella, 30, Bloomfield, N.J.
World Trade Center

Mario Nardone
World Trade Center

Shawn Nassaney, 25, Pawtucket, R.I.
United Flight 175 - WTC, airline passenger

Karen Navarro, 30, Bayside, N.Y.
World Trade Center

Joseph Navas, 44, Paramus, N.J.
World Trade Center

Francis Nazario, 28, Jersey City, N.J.
World Trade Center

Marcus Neblett, 31
World Trade Center

Laurence Nedell, 52
World Trade Center

Luke Nee, 44, Stony Point, N.Y.
World Trade Center

Pete Negron, Bergenfield, N.J.
World Trade Center

Laurie Neira
American Flight 11 - WTC, airline passenger

Ann Nelson, 30
World Trade Center

David W. Nelson
World Trade Center

James Nelson, 40, Clark, N.J.
World Trade Center

Peter Nelson
World Trade Center

Gerard Nevins
World Trade Center

Renee Newell, 37, Cranston, R.I.
American Flight 11 - WTC, airline passenger

Christopher Newton, 38, Ashburn, Va.
American Flight 77 - Pentagon, airline passenger

Khang Nguyen, 41, Fairfax, Va.
Pentagon

Kathleen Nicosia
American Flight 11 - WTC, flight crew

Alfonse Niedermeyer, Manasquan, N.J.
World Trade Center

Martin Nierderer, 23, Hoboken, N.J.
World Trade Center

Gloria Nieves
World Trade Center, Colombian

Paul R. Nimbley, 42, Middletown, N.J.
World Trade Center

John Ballantine Niven, 44, New York, N.Y.
World Trade Center

Michael Allen Noeth, 30, New York, N.Y.
Pentagon

Daniel Nolan, 44, Lake Hopatcong, N.J.
World Trade Center

Robert Walter Noonan, 36, Norwalk, Conn.
World Trade Center

Jacqueline Norton, 60, Lubec, Maine
American Flight 11 - WTC, airline passenger

Robert Norton, 82, Lubec, Maine
American Flight 11 - WTC, airline passenger

Daniela R. Notaro
World Trade Center

Soichi Numata, 45
World Trade Center, Japanese

Jose Nunez, 42
World Trade Center

Jeffrey Nussbaum
World Trade Center

Dennis Oberg
World Trade Center

Michael O'Brien, 42, Cedar Knolls, N.J.
World Trade Center

Timothy O'Brien, 40, Rockville Centre, N.Y.
World Trade Center

Lt. Daniel O'Callaghan
World Trade Center

Jefferson Ocampo, 28
World Trade Center, Colombian

Diana O'Connor
World Trade Center

Keith K. O'Connor, 28, Hoboken, N.J.
World Trade Center

Richard J. O'Connor, 48, LaGrangeville, N.Y.
World Trade Center

Amy O'Doherty, 23, New York, N.Y.
World Trade Center

Marni Pont O'Doherty, 31, Armonk, N.Y.
World Trade Center

Douglas Oelschlager
World Trade Center

Philip Ognibene
World Trade Center

John Ogonowski, 52, Dracut, Mass.
American Flight 11 - WTC, flight crew

James Andrew O'Grady, 32, Harrington Park, N.J.
World Trade Center

Joseph Ogren
World Trade Center

Lt. Thomas O'Hagan
World Trade Center

Samuel Oitice
World Trade Center

Patrick O'Keefe, 44, Oakdale, N.Y.
World Trade Center

Capt. William O'Keefe, 49
World Trade Center

Gerald O'Leary, 34
World Trade Center

Linda Oliva
World Trade Center

Edward K. Oliver, 31, Jackson, N.J.
World Trade Center

Eric Olsen
World Trade Center

Jeffrey Olsen
World Trade Center

Barbara Olson, 45
American Flight 77 - Pentagon, airline passenger

Maureen Olson, 50, Rockville Centre, N.Y.
World Trade Center

Steven Olson
World Trade Center

Matthew O'Mahoney, Philmont, N.Y.
World Trade Center

Toshihiro Onda, 39
World Trade Center, Japanese

John P. O'Neill, 49
World Trade Center

Peter J. O'Neill, 21, Amityville, N.Y.
World Trade Center

Sean Gordon Corbett O'Neill, 34, Rye, N.Y.
World Trade Center

Betty Ong, 45, Andover, Mass.
American Flight 11 - WTC, flight crew

Michael Opperman, 45
World Trade Center

Chris Orgielewicz
World Trade Center

Margaret Orloske, 50, Windsor, Conn.
World Trade Center

Virginia Ormiston-Kenworthy, New York, N.Y.
World Trade Center

Ruben Ornedo, 39, Los Angeles, Calif.
American Flight 77 - Pentagon, airline passenger

Kevin O'Rourke, 44
World Trade Center

Juan Romero Orozco
World Trade Center

Peter K. Ortale, 37, New York, N.Y.
World Trade Center

Jane Orth, 49, Haverhill, Mass.
American Flight 11 - WTC, airline passenger

David Ortiz, Nanuet, N.Y.
World Trade Center

Emilio (Peter) Ortiz
World Trade Center

Masaru Ose, 36
World Trade Center, Japanese

Patrick J. O'Shea
World Trade Center

Robert W. O'Shea, 47, Wall, N.J.
World Trade Center

James Robert Ostrowski, 37, Garden City, N.Y.
World Trade Center

Timothy O'Sullivan, 68, Albrightsville, Pa.
World Trade Center

Jason Oswald, 28, New York, N.Y.
World Trade Center

Michael Otten
World Trade Center

Todd Ouida, 25, River Edge, N.J.
World Trade Center

Peter J. Owens, Williston Park, N.Y.
World Trade Center

Diana B. Padro, 55, Woodbridge, Va.
Pentagon

Spc. Chin Sun Pak, 25, Okla.
Pentagon

Deepa K. Pakkala, 31, Stewartsville, N.J.
World Trade Center

Jeffrey Palazzo
World Trade Center

Thomas Anthony Palazzo, 44, Armonk, N.Y.
World Trade Center

Richard Palazzolo
World Trade Center

Orio Palmer
World Trade Center

Frank Palombo
World Trade Center

Alan Palumbo
World Trade Center

Lt. Jonas Martin Panik, 26, Mingoville, Pa.
Pentagon

Paul Pansini
World Trade Center

John Paolillo
World Trade Center

Edward J. Papa, 47, Oyster Bay, N.Y.
World Trade Center

Salvatore Papasso, 34, Annadale, N.Y.
World Trade Center

James Pappageorge
World Trade Center

Marie Pappalardo
United Flight 175 - WTC, airline passenger

Vinod K. Parakat, 34, Sayreville, N.J.
World Trade Center

Vijayashanker Paramsothy, 23
World Trade Center

Hardai (Casey) Parbhu, 42
World Trade Center

James Parham, New York, N.Y.
World Trade Center

Debbie Paris
World Trade Center

Philip L. Parker, 53, Skillman, N.J.
World Trade Center

Robert Emmett Parks, 47, Middletown, N.J.
World Trade Center

Hasmukh Parmar, 48, N.J.
World Trade Center

Robert Parro
World Trade Center

Diane Parsons, 58, Malta, N.Y.
World Trade Center

Leobardo Lopez Pascual, 41, New York, N.Y.
World Trade Center

Michael J. Pascuma, 50, Massapequa Park, N.Y.
World Trade Center

Jerrold Paskins, 57, Anaheim Hills, Calif.
World Trade Center

Suzanne Passaro, 42
World Trade Center

Avnish Patel
World Trade Center

Dipti Patel
World Trade Center

Manish K. Patel, 29, Edison, N.J.
World Trade Center

Steven B. Paterson, 40, Ridgewood, N.J.
World Trade Center

James Patrick, 30, Norwalk, Conn.
World Trade Center

Manuel Patrocino, 34
World Trade Center

Bernard E. Patterson, 46, Upper Brookville, N.Y.
World Trade Center

Maj. Clifford L. Patterson, 33, Alexandria, Va.
Pentagon

Cira Marie Patti, 40, New York, N.Y.
World Trade Center

James R. Paul, New York, N.Y.
World Trade Center

Patrice Paz
World Trade Center

Victor Paz-Gutierrez
World Trade Center, Colombian

Stacey L. Peak, 36, New York, N.Y.
World Trade Center

Durrell Pearsall
World Trade Center

Thomas Pecorelli, 31, Los Angeles, Calif.
American Flight 11 - WTC, airline passenger

Thomas E. Pedecini
World Trade Center

Todd D. Pelino, 34, Fair Haven, N.J.
World Trade Center

Angel R. Pena, 45, River Vale, N.J.
World Trade Center

Robert Penniger, 63, Poway, Calif.
American Flight 77 - Pentagon, airline passenger

Robert David Peraza, 30, New York, N.Y.
World Trade Center

Maria Percoco
World Trade Center

Jon A. Perconti, 32, Brick, N.J.
World Trade Center

Angel Perez, 43, Jersey City, N.J.
World Trade Center

Angela Susan Perez, 35, New York, N.Y.
World Trade Center

Anthony Perez
World Trade Center

Nancy E. Perez, Union City, N.J.
World Trade Center

Berry Berenson Perkins, 53, Wellfleet, Mass.
American Flight 11 - WTC, airline passenger

Emelda Perry
World Trade Center

Lt. Glenn Perry
World Trade Center

Frank Pershep, 59
World Trade Center

Michael J. Pescherine, 32, New York, N.Y.
World Trade Center

Donald A. Peterson, 66, Spring Lake, N.J.
United Flight 93 - Pennsylvania, airline passenger

Jean Hoadley Peterson, 55, Spring Lake, N.J.
United Flight 93 - Pennsylvania, airline passenger

Mark Petrocelli, 29, New York, N.Y.
World Trade Center

Lt. Philip Petti
World Trade Center

Dominick Pezzulo, 36, New York, N.Y.
World Trade Center

Kaleen E. Pezzuti, 28, Fair Haven, N.J.
World Trade Center

Lt. Kevin Pfeifer
World Trade Center

Tu-Anh Pham
World Trade Center

Lt. Kenneth Phelan
World Trade Center

Ludwig J. Picarro, 44, Basking Ridge, N.J.
World Trade Center

Matthew Picerno, 44, Holmdel, N.J.
World Trade Center

Christopher Pickford
World Trade Center

Bernard T. Pietronico, 39, Old Bridge, N.J.
World Trade Center

Nicholas P. Pietrunti, 38, Belford, N.J.
World Trade Center

Joseph Piskaldo, 48, North Arlington, N.J.
World Trade Center

Todd Pitman, 30, New York, N.Y.
World Trade Center

Josh Piver
World Trade Center

Robert R. Ploger, 59, Annandale, Va.
American Flight 77 - Pentagon, airline passenger

Joseph Plumitallo, 45, Manalapan, N.J.
World Trade Center

John M. Pocher, 36, Middletown, N.J.
World Trade Center

William H. Pohlmann, 56, Ardsley, N.Y.
World Trade Center

Laurence Polatsch, 32, New York, N.Y.
World Trade Center

Thomas Polhemus, 39, Parsippany, N.J.
World Trade Center

Steve Pollicino, 48, Hicksville, N.Y.
World Trade Center

Susan Pollio
World Trade Center

Lt. J.G. Darin Howard Pontell, 26, Columbia, Md.
Pentagon

Joshua Poptean, 37, N.Y.
World Trade Center

Anthony Portillo
World Trade Center

James E. Potorti, 52, Plainsboro, N.J.
World Trade Center

Daphne Pouletsos, 47, Westwood, N.J.
World Trade Center

Stephen Poulos, 45
World Trade Center

Scott Powell, 35, Silver Spring, Md.
Pentagon

Shawn Powell
World Trade Center

Gregory M. Preziose, 34, Holmdel, N.J.
World Trade Center

Vincent Princiotta
World Trade Center

Kevin Prior, 28
World Trade Center

Carrie Progen, 24
World Trade Center

David L. Pruim, 53, Upper Montclair, N.J.
World Trade Center

Richard Prunty, 57, Sayville, N.Y.
World Trade Center

John F. Puckett, 47, Glen Cove, N.Y.
World Trade Center

Edward Pullis, 34, Hazlet, N.J.
World Trade Center

Patricia Ann Puma, 33, New York, N.Y.
World Trade Center

(Retired) Capt. Jack Punches, 51, Clifton, Va.
Pentagon

Sonia Morales Puopolo, 58, Dover, Mass.
American Flight 11 - WTC, airline passenger

Joseph John Pycior, 39, Carlstadt, N.J.
Pentagon

Edward R. Pykon, 33, Princeton Junction, N.J.
World Trade Center

Christopher Quackenbush, 44, Manhasset, N.Y.
World Trade Center

Lincoln Quappe
World Trade Center

Patrick Quigley, 40, Wellesley, Mass.
United Flight 175 - WTC, airline passenger

Lt. Michael Quilty
World Trade Center

Ricardo Quinn
World Trade Center

Carol Rabalais, 38
World Trade Center

Leonard Ragaglia
World Trade Center

Eugene J. Raggio, New York, N.Y.
World Trade Center

Michael Ragusa
World Trade Center

Peter F. Raimondi
World Trade Center

Harry Raines, 37, Bethpage, N.Y.
World Trade Center

Lisa J. Raines, 42, Great Falls, Va.
American Flight 77 - Pentagon, airline passenger

Valsa Raju
World Trade Center

Edward Rall
World Trade Center

Maria Isabel Ramirez, 25, New York, N.Y.
World Trade Center

Harry Ramos, 45, Newark, N.J.
World Trade Center

Deborah Ramsaur, 45, Annandale, Va.
Pentagon

Alfred T. Rancke, 42, Summit, N.J.
World Trade Center

Todd Rancke
World Trade Center

Adam Rand
World Trade Center

Shreyes Ranganath, 26, N.J.
World Trade Center

Rhonda Rasmussen, 44, Woodbridge, Va.
Pentagon

Robert Arthur Rasmussen, 42, Hinsdale, Ill.
World Trade Center

Roger (Mark) Rasweiler, 53, Flemington, N.J.
World Trade Center

Marsha Dianah Ratchford, 34, Prichard, Ala.
Pentagon

David Alan James Rathkey, 47, Mountain Lakes, N.J.
World Trade Center

William R. Raub, 38, Saddle River, N.J.
World Trade Center

Alexey Razuvaev
World Trade Center

Michele Reed, 26, N.J.
World Trade Center

Judith A. Reese, 56, Kearny, N.J.
World Trade Center

Donald Regan
World Trade Center

Lt. Robert Regan
World Trade Center

Thomas M. Regan, 43, Cranford, N.J.
World Trade Center

Christian Regenhard
World Trade Center

Gregory Reidy, 25, Holmdel, N.J.
World Trade Center

James Reilly, 25
World Trade Center

Kevin Reilly
World Trade Center

Timothy E. Reilly, 40, New York, N.Y.
World Trade Center

Thomas Barnes Reinig, 48, Bernardsville, N.J.
World Trade Center

Frank B. Reisman, 41, Princeton, N.J.
World Trade Center

Joshua Scott Reiss, 23, New York, N.Y.
World Trade Center

John Armand Reo, 28, Larchmont, N.Y.
World Trade Center

Richard Rescoroa, 62, N.J.
World Trade Center

John Resta
World Trade Center

Martha Reszke, 36, Stafford, Va.
Pentagon

David Retik, Needham, Mass.
American Flight 11 - WTC, airline passenger

Todd Reuben, 40, Potomac, Md.
American Flight 77 - Pentagon, airline passenger

Luis C. Revilla
World Trade Center

Bruce Reynolds, Columbia, N.J.
World Trade Center

Frederick Rhodes, 57, N.J.
World Trade Center

John Rhodes, 57
World Trade Center

Francis S. Riccardelli, Westwood, N.J.
World Trade Center

David Rice, 31, New York, N.Y.
World Trade Center

Cecelia E. Richard, 41, Fort Washington, Md.
Pentagon

Lt. Vernon Richard
World Trade Center

Michael Richards, 38
World Trade Center

Venesha Richards, North Brunswick, N.J.
World Trade Center

James Riches
World Trade Center

Frederick Rimmele, 32, Marblehead, Mass.
United Flight 175 - WTC, airline passenger

Ginger Risco
World Trade Center

Joseph Rivelli
World Trade Center

Isaias Rivera, 51, Perth Amboy, N.J.
World Trade Center

Joseph R. Riverso, 34, White Plains, N.Y.
World Trade Center

Paul Rizza, 34, Park Ridge, N.J.
World Trade Center

Stephen L. Roach, 37, Verona, N.J.
World Trade Center

Joseph Roberto
World Trade Center

Leo Roberts, 44, Wayne, N.J.
World Trade Center

Michael Roberts
World Trade Center

Donald W. Robertson, 38, Rumson, N.J.
World Trade Center

Jeffrey Robinson, 38, South Brunswick, N.J.
World Trade Center

Michell Robotham, 32
World Trade Center

Donald Robson, 52, Manhasset, N.Y.
World Trade Center

Antonio Augusto Tome Rocha, 34, East Hanover, N.J.
World Trade Center, Portugese

John M. Rodak, 39, Sewell, N.J.
World Trade Center

Anthony Rodriguez
World Trade Center

Antonio Jose Carrusca Rodriguez, Port Washington,
N.Y.
World Trade Center, Portugese

Carlos Cortez Rodriguez
World Trade Center, Colombian

Carmen Rodriguez, 46
World Trade Center

Gregory Rodriguez
World Trade Center

Richard Rodriguez, Cliffwood, N.J.
World Trade Center

Matthew Rogan, 37, West Islip, N.Y.
World Trade Center

Jean Roger, 24, Longmeadow, Mass.
American Flight 11 - WTC, flight crew

Scott Rohner, 22
World Trade Center

Elvin Santiago Romero, New York, N.Y.
World Trade Center

James Romito, Westwood, N.J.
World Trade Center

Eric Ropiteau
World Trade Center

Aida Rosario, 42, Jersey City, N.J.
World Trade Center

Mark Rosen, 45, West Islip, N.Y.
World Trade Center

Sheryl L. Rosenbaum, 33, Warren Township, N.J.
World Trade Center

Linda Rosenbaun, 41, Little Falls, N.J.
World Trade Center

Lloyd D. Rosenberg, 31, Marlboro, N.J.
World Trade Center

Joshua Rosenblum
World Trade Center

Josh Rosenthal, 43
World Trade Center

Richard D. Rosenthal, 50, Fair Lawn, N.J.
World Trade Center

Philip Rosenzweig, Acton, Mass.
American Flight 11 - WTC, airline passenger

Richard Ross, 58, Newton, Mass.
American Flight 11 - WTC, airline passenger

Daniel Rossetti, 32, Bloomfield, N.J.
World Trade Center

Norman Rossinow, 39
World Trade Center

Nicholas Rossomando
World Trade Center

Mike Rothberg, 39, Old Greenwich, Conn.
World Trade Center

Donna Rothenberg, 53
World Trade Center

Mark Rothenberg, Scotch Plains, N.J.
United Flight 93 - Pennsylvania, airline passenger

James M. Roux, 43, Portland, Maine
United Flight 175 - WTC, airline passenger

Nick Rowe, 29, Hoboken, N.J.
World Trade Center

Edward V. Rowenhorst, 32, Lake Ridge, Va.
Pentagon

Judy Rowlett, 44, Woodbridge, Va.
Pentagon

Paul Ruback
World Trade Center

Ronald J. Ruben
World Trade Center

Susan Ann Ruggiero, 30, Plainview, N.Y.
World Trade Center

Gilbert Ruiz, 45, New York, N.Y.
World Trade Center

Robert E. Russell, 52, Oxon Hill, Md.
Pentagon

Stephen Russell
World Trade Center

Steven H. Russin, 32, Mendham, N.J.
World Trade Center

Lt. Michael Russo
World Trade Center

William R. Ruth, 57, Md.
Pentagon

Edward Ryan
World Trade Center

John J. Ryan, 45, West Windsor, N.J.
World Trade Center

Jonathan S. Ryan
World Trade Center

Kristy Irvine Ryan
World Trade Center

Matthew Ryan
World Trade Center

Christina Ryook
World Trade Center

Jason Sabbag, 26, Greenwich, Conn.
World Trade Center

Thomas Sabella, 44, Willowbrook, N.Y.
World Trade Center

Scott Saber, 38
World Trade Center

Charles E. Sabin, Burke, Va.
Pentagon

Jessica Sachs, 22, Billerica, Mass.
American Flight 11 - WTC, airline passenger

Francis Sadocha, 41, Huntington, N.Y.
World Trade Center

Brock Safronoff, 26
World Trade Center

John Salamone, 37, North Caldwell, N.J.
World Trade Center

Marjorie C. Salamone, 53, Springfield, Va.
Pentagon

Hernando Salas
World Trade Center, Colombian

John S. Salerno, 31, Westfield, N.J.
World Trade Center

Rahma Salie, 28, Boston, Mass.
American Flight 11 - WTC, airline passenger

Richard L. Salinardi, 32, Hoboken, N.J.
World Trade Center

Wayne Saloman
World Trade Center

Catherine Salter, 37
World Trade Center

Frank Salvaterra, 41, Manhasset, N.Y.
World Trade Center

Paul Salvio
World Trade Center

Samuel R. Salvo
World Trade Center

John Sammartino, 37, Annandale, Va.
American Flight 77 - Pentagon, airline passenger

James K. Samuel
World Trade Center

James T. Samuel, 29, Jamesburg, N.J.
World Trade Center

Michael V. San Phillip, 55, Ridgewood, N.J.
World Trade Center

Sylvia San Pio, 27
World Trade Center

Hugo Sanay-Perafiel
World Trade Center

Jesus Sanchez, 45, Hudson, Mass.
United Flight 175 - WTC, airline passenger

Eric Sand, 36
World Trade Center

Herman Sandler, 57
World Trade Center

James Sands, 38, Brick, N.J.
World Trade Center

Maria Santillan, 27, Morris Plains, N.J.
World Trade Center

Christopher Santora
World Trade Center

John Santore, 49, New York, N.Y.
World Trade Center

Rafael Humberto Santos
World Trade Center, Colombian

Victor J. Saracini, 51, Lower Makefield Township, Pa.
United Flight 175 - WTC, flight crew

Kalyan K. Sarkar, 54, Westwood, N.J.
World Trade Center

Paul F. Sarle, 38, Babylon Village, N.Y.
World Trade Center

Deepika K. Sattaluri, 33, Edison, N.J.
World Trade Center

Gregory Saucedo
World Trade Center

Susan Sauer, 48
World Trade Center

Anthony Savas, Astoria, N.Y.
World Trade Center

Jackie Sayegh, 34
World Trade Center

Dawn Elizabeth Scala, 31, Millville, N.J.
World Trade Center

Lt. Col. David M. Scales, 45, Cleveland, Ohio
Pentagon

Robert Scandole, 37
World Trade Center

Michelle Scarpitta
World Trade Center

Dennis Scauso
World Trade Center

John Schardt
World Trade Center

Fred Scheffold, Piermont, N.Y.
World Trade Center

Scott M. Schertzer, 28, Edison, N.J.
World Trade Center

Sean Schielke, 27, New York, N.Y.
World Trade Center

Steven Schlag, 41, Franklin Lakes, N.J.
World Trade Center

Cmdr. Robert Allan Schlegel, 38, Gray, Maine
Pentagon

Ian Schneider, 45, Short Hills, N.J.
World Trade Center

Thomas Schoales
World Trade Center

Gerard Schrang, 45
World Trade Center

John Schroeder
World Trade Center

Edward W. Schunk
World Trade Center

Clarin Schwartz, 51
World Trade Center

John Schwartz
World Trade Center

Mark Schwartz, 50
World Trade Center

Adriane Scibetta
World Trade Center

Raphael Scorca, 61, Beachwood, N.J.
World Trade Center

Janice Scott, 46, Springfield, Va.
Pentagon

Randolph Scott, 48, Stamford, Conn.
World Trade Center

Jason Sekzer
World Trade Center

Matthew Sellitto, 23, New Vernon, N.J.
World Trade Center

Michael Selves, 53, Fairfax, Va.
Pentagon

Howard Selwyn
World Trade Center

Larry Senko, 34, Lower Makefield Township, Pa.
World Trade Center

Frankie Serrano, 23, Elizabeth, N.J.
World Trade Center

Marian Serva, 47, Stafford, Va.
Pentagon

Karen Seymour-Dietrich, 40, Millington, N.J.
World Trade Center

Davis (Deeg) Sezna, 22
World Trade Center

Jayesh Shah, 38
World Trade Center

Khalid M. Shahid, 25, Union, N.J.
World Trade Center

Cmdr. Dan Frederic Shanower, 40, Naperville, Ill.
Pentagon

Kadaba Shashikiran, 26, Hackensack, N.J.
World Trade Center

Barbara A. Shaw, 57, Morris Township, N.J.
World Trade Center

Daniel James Shea, 37, Pelham, N.Y.
World Trade Center

Joseph Patrick Shea, 47, Pelham, N.Y.
World Trade Center

Kathleen Shearer, 61, Dover, N.H.
United Flight 175 - WTC, airline passenger

Michael Shearer, 63, Dover, N.H.
United Flight 175 - WTC, airline passenger

Linda Sheehan
World Trade Center

Hagay Shefi, 34, Israel
World Trade Center

Antoinette Sherman, 35, Forest Heights, Md.
Pentagon

John A. Sherry
World Trade Center

Mark Shulman, 47, Old Bridge, N.J.
World Trade Center

See-Wong Shun, 44, Westfield, N.J.
World Trade Center

Carmen Sierra, 46, Orange, N.J.
World Trade Center

Johanna Sigmund
World Trade Center

Dianne Signer
World Trade Center

Gregory Sikorsky
World Trade Center

Stephen Siller, 34, West Brighton, N.Y.
World Trade Center

David Silver, 35
World Trade Center

Craig Silverstein
World Trade Center

Bruce E. Simmons, 41, Ridgewood, N.J.
World Trade Center

Diane Simmons
American Flight 77 - Pentagon, airline passenger

Don Simmons, 58, Dumfries, Va.
Pentagon

George Simmons
American Flight 77 - Pentagon, airline passenger

Artie Simon
World Trade Center

Kenneth Simon, 34, Secaucus, N.J.
World Trade Center

Michael John Simon, 40, Harrington Park, N.J.
World Trade Center

Marianne Simone
World Trade Center

Jane Simpkin, 35, Wayland, Mass.
United Flight 175 - WTC, airline passenger

Cheryle Sincock, 53, Dale City, Va.
Pentagon

Khamladai Singh, 25, New York, N.Y.
World Trade Center

Roshan Singh, 21, New York, N.Y.
World Trade Center

Thomas Sinton, 41, Croton on Hudson, N.Y.
World Trade Center

Peter A. Siracuse, 29, New York, N.Y.
World Trade Center

Muriel F. Siskopoulos
World Trade Center

Joseph M. Sisolak, 35, New York, N.Y.
World Trade Center

John Skala, Clifton, N.J.
World Trade Center

Francis J. Skidmore, 58, Randolph, N.J.
World Trade Center

Toyena C. Skinner, 27, Kingston, N.J.
World Trade Center

Paul Skrzypek, 37
World Trade Center

Christopher Slattery, 31, New York, N.Y.
World Trade Center

Vincent Slavin, Rockaway, N.Y.
World Trade Center

Vincent Slavin, Rockaway, N.Y.
World Trade Center

Robert Sliwak, Wantagh, N.Y.
World Trade Center

Paul K. Sloan
World Trade Center

Stanley Smagala
World Trade Center

Gregg Harold Smallwood, 44, Overland Park, Kan.
Pentagon

Cathy T. Smith, 44, West Haverstraw, N.Y.
World Trade Center

Daniel L. Smith, 47, Northport, N.Y.
World Trade Center

(Retired) Lt. Col. Gary F. Smith, 55, Alexandria, Va.
Pentagon

Heather Smith, 30, Boston, Mass.
American Flight 11 - WTC, airline passenger

James G. Smith, Garden City, N.Y.
World Trade Center

Jeffrey Smith
World Trade Center

Karl Trumbull Smith, 44, Little Silver, N.J.
World Trade Center

Kevin Smith
World Trade Center

Leon Smith
World Trade Center

Bonnie Smithwick
World Trade Center

Christine Snyder, 32, Kailua, Hawaii
United Flight 93 - Pennsylvania, airline passenger

Dianne Snyder, 42, Westport, Mass.
American Flight 11 - WTC, flight crew

Leonard J. Snyder, 38, Cranford, N.J.
World Trade Center

Astrid E. Sohan, 32, Freehold, N.J.
World Trade Center

Dan W. Song, 34
World Trade Center

Mari-Rae Sopper, 35, Santa Barbara, Calif.
American Flight 77 - Pentagon, airline passenger

Michael Sorresse, 34, Morris Plains, N.J.
World Trade Center

Stephen Soulas, 45, Basking Ridge, N.J.
World Trade Center

Timothy P. Soulas, West Chester, Pa.
World Trade Center

Gregory T. Spagnoletti
World Trade Center

Donald Spampinato
World Trade Center

Thomas Sparacio
World Trade Center

Robert Spear
World Trade Center

Robert Speisman, 47, Irvington, N.Y.
American Flight 77 - Pentagon, airline passenger

George Spencer, 50, West Norwalk, Conn.
World Trade Center

Robert A. Spencer, 35, Middletown, N.J.
World Trade Center

Frank J. Spinelli, 44, Short Hills, N.J.
World Trade Center

Will Spitz
World Trade Center

Joseph Spor
World Trade Center

Micheal Stabile
World Trade Center

Lawrence Stack
World Trade Center

Capt. Timothy Stackpole, 42, New York, N.Y.
World Trade Center

Richard James Stadelberger, 55, Middletown, N.J.
World Trade Center

Eric A. Stahlman, 43, Holmdel Township, N.J.
World Trade Center

Gregory Stajk
World Trade Center

Corina Stan, 31
World Trade Center

Anthony M. Starita, 35, Westfield, N.J.
World Trade Center

Jeffrey Stark, 30, Great Kills, N.Y.
World Trade Center

Derek J. Statkevicus, 30, Norwalk, Conn.
World Trade Center

Patricia J. Statz, 41, Takoma Park, Md.
Pentagon

Craig W. Staub, 30, Basking Ridge, N.J.
World Trade Center

Eric Steen, 32
World Trade Center

Alexander Robbins Steinman, 32, Hoboken, N.J.
World Trade Center

Edna L. Stephens, 53, Washington, D.C.
Pentagon

Andrew Stern, 45, Bellmore, N.Y.
World Trade Center

Norma Lang Steuerle, 54, Alexandria, Va.
American Flight 77 - Pentagon, airline passenger

Michael J. Stewart
World Trade Center

Richard H. Stewart, 35, New York, N.Y.
World Trade Center

Douglas Stone, 54, Dover, N.H.
American Flight 11 - WTC, airline passenger

Lonny J. Stone
World Trade Center

Jimmy Nevill Storey, 58, Katy, Texas
World Trade Center

Timothy Stout, 42, Dobbs Ferry, N.Y.
World Trade Center

Thomas S. Strada, Chatham, N.J.
World Trade Center

James J. Straine, 36, Oceanport, N.J.
World Trade Center

George Strauch
World Trade Center

George L. Straunch, 53, Avon-by-the-Sea, N.J.
World Trade Center

Edward T. Strauss, 44, Edison, N.J.
World Trade Center

Sgt. Maj. Larry Strickland, 52, Woodbridge, Va.
Pentagon

Steven Strobert, 33, Ridgewood, N.J.
World Trade Center

Walwyn Stuart, Valley Stream, N.Y.
World Trade Center

Benjamin Suarez
World Trade Center

David S. Suarez, 24, West Windsor, N.J.
World Trade Center

Xavier Suarez
American Flight 11 - WTC, airline passenger

Yoichi Sugiyama, 34
World Trade Center, Japanese

Daniel Suhr, 37, Neponsit, N.Y.
World Trade Center

Lt. Christopher Sullivan
World Trade Center

Patrick Sullivan, Breezy Point, N.Y.
World Trade Center

Thomas Sullivan, 38, Kearney, N.J.
World Trade Center

Colleen Supinski
World Trade Center

Robert Sutcliffe, 39, Huntington, N.Y.
World Trade Center

Selina Sutter, 58, Chatham, N.J.
World Trade Center

Brian D. Sweeney, 38, Barnstable, Mass.
United Flight 175 - WTC, airline passenger

Madeline Sweeney, 35, Acton, Mass.
American Flight 11 - WTC, flight crew

Kenneth J. Swenson, 30, Chatham, N.J.
World Trade Center

Thomas F. Swift, 30, Jersey City, N.J.
World Trade Center

Derek O. Sword
World Trade Center

Kevin T. Szocik, 27
World Trade Center

Joann Tabeek, 41
World Trade Center

Michael Taddonio, 39, Huntington, N.Y.
World Trade Center

Keiichiro Takahashi, 53
World Trade Center, Japanese

Keiji Takahashi, 42, Tenafly, N.J.
World Trade Center, Japanese

Robert R. Talhami, 40, Shrewsbury, N.J.
World Trade Center

John Talignani, 72, New York, N.Y.
United Flight 93 - Pennsylvania, airline passenger

Sean Tallon
World Trade Center

Michael Andrew Tamuccio, 37, Pelham Manor, N.Y.
World Trade Center

Kenichiro Tanaka, 52
World Trade Center, Japanese

Rhondelle Cherie Tankard, 31
World Trade Center

Michael Tanner, Secaucus, N.J.
World Trade Center

Dennis Taormina, 36, N.J.
World Trade Center

Kenneth Joseph Tarantino, 39, Bayonne, N.J.
World Trade Center

Allan Tarasiewicz
World Trade Center

Michael Tarrou, 38, Stafford Springs, Conn.
United Flight 175 - WTC, flight crew

Ron Tartaro
World Trade Center

Donnie Taylor, 40
World Trade Center

Hilda E. Taylor, 62, Forestville, Md.
American Flight 77 - Pentagon, airline passenger

Maj. Kip P. Taylor, 38, McLean, Va.
Pentagon

Leonard Taylor, 44, Reston, Va.
American Flight 77 - Pentagon, airline passenger

Sandra Taylor, 50, Alexandria, Va.
Pentagon

Sandra Teague, 31, Fairfax, Va.
American Flight 77 - Pentagon, airline passenger

Karl W. Teepe, Centreville, Va.
Pentagon

Paul Tegtmeier
World Trade Center

Yesh Tembe, 59, Piscataway, N.J.
World Trade Center

Anthony Tempesta, 38, Elizabeth, N.J.
World Trade Center

David Tengelin, 25, Goteborg, Sweden
World Trade Center, Swedish

Brian Terrenzi
World Trade Center

Michael Theodoridis, 32, Boston, Mass.
American Flight 11 - WTC, airline passenger

Thomas F. Theurkauf, 44, Stamford, Conn.
World Trade Center

Lesley Thomas
World Trade Center

Clive Thompson, 43, Summit, N.J.
World Trade Center

Glenn Thompson, 44, New York, N.Y.
World Trade Center

Nigel Bruce Thompson, 33, New York, N.Y.
World Trade Center

Perry Anthony Thompson, 36, Mount Laurel, N.J.
World Trade Center

Eric R. Thorpe
World Trade Center

Nichola A. Thorpe
World Trade Center

Sgt. Tamara Thurman, 25, Brewton, Ala.
Pentagon

Sal Tieri, 40, Shrewsbury, N.J.
World Trade Center

John Patrick Tierney, 27
World Trade Center

Kenneth Tietjen, 31, Matawan, N.J.
World Trade Center

Stephen Tighe
World Trade Center

Scott Timmes
World Trade Center

Michael Tinley, 56, Dallas, Texas
World Trade Center

Jennifer M. Tino, 29, West Caldwell, N.J.
World Trade Center

Robert Tipaldi
World Trade Center

John Tipping
World Trade Center

Hector Tirado
World Trade Center

Alicia N. Titus, 28, San Francisco, Calif.
United Flight 175 - WTC, flight crew

John J. Tobin, 47, Kenilworth, N.J.
World Trade Center

Richard J. Todisco, 61, Wyckoff, N.J.
World Trade Center

Lt. Cmdr. Otis Vincent Tolbert, 38, Lemoore, Calif.
Pentagon

Steve Tompsett
World Trade Center

Doris Torres, 32
World Trade Center

Luis Torres, 31
World Trade Center, Colombian

Christophe M. Traina, 25, Brick, N.J.
World Trade Center

Wally P. Travers, 44, Upper Saddle River, N.J.
World Trade Center

James Trentini, 65, Everett, Mass.
American Flight 11 - WTC, airline passenger

Mary Trentini, 67, Everett, Mass.
American Flight 11 - WTC, airline passenger

Lisa L. Trerotola, Hazlet, N.J.
World Trade Center

Gregory J. Trost
World Trade Center

Willie Q. Troy, 51, Aberdeen Proving Ground, Md.
Pentagon

William Tselepis, 33, New Providence, N.J.
World Trade Center

Zhanetta Tsoy, 32, Jersey City, N.J.
World Trade Center

Michael Patrick Tucker, 40, Rumson, N.J.
World Trade Center

Lance Richard Tumulty, 32, Bridgewater, N.J.
World Trade Center

Jennifer Tzemis
World Trade Center

John G. Ueltzhoeffer, 36, Roselle Park, N.J.
World Trade Center

Tyler Ugolyn, 23, Ridgefield, Conn.
World Trade Center

Michael A. Uliano, 42, Aberdeen, N.J.
World Trade Center

Jonathan Uman, 33, Westport, Conn.
World Trade Center

Anil S. Umarkar, 34, Hackensack, N.J.
World Trade Center

John Damien Vaccacio, 30, New York, N.Y.
World Trade Center

Bradley H. Vadas, 37, Westport, Conn.
World Trade Center

Mayra Valdes-Rodriguez, 39
World Trade Center

Santos Valentin
World Trade Center

Pendyala Vamsikrishna, 30, Los Angeles, Calif.
American Flight 11 - WTC, airline passenger

Erica Van Acker
World Trade Center

Kenneth W. Van Auken, 47, East Brunswick, N.J.
World Trade Center

Jon C. Vandevander, 44, Ridgewood, N.J.
World Trade Center

Richard Vanhine
World Trade Center

Daniel M. VanLaere, 46, Glen Rock, N.J.
World Trade Center

Frederick Varacchi, 35, Greenwich, Conn.
World Trade Center

Scott C. Vasel, 32, Park Ridge, N.J.
World Trade Center

Lt. Cmdr. Ronald James Vauk, 37, Nampa, Idaho
Pentagon

Peter Vega
World Trade Center

Sankara Velamuri, 63, Avenel, N.J.
World Trade Center

Jorge Velazquez, 47, Passaic, N.J.
World Trade Center

Lawrence Veling
World Trade Center

Anthony M. Ventura, 41, Middletown, N.J.
World Trade Center

David Vera
World Trade Center

Christopher Vialonga, 30, Demerest, N.J.
World Trade Center

Matthew Vianna
World Trade Center

John Vigiano
World Trade Center

Frank J. Vignola
World Trade Center

Joseph B. Vilardo, 42, Stanhope, N.J.
World Trade Center

Sergio Villanueva
World Trade Center

Melissa Vincent, 28, Hoboken, N.J.
World Trade Center

Francine Virgilio, 48, New York, N.Y.
World Trade Center

Lawrence Virgilio
World Trade Center

Joseph G. Visciano
World Trade Center

Richard Vito, 54, Manalapan, N.J.
World Trade Center

Gregory Wachtler, 25, N.J.
World Trade Center

Lt. Col. Karen Wagner, 40, Texas
Pentagon

Mary Wahlstrom, 75, Kaysville, Utah
American Flight 11 - WTC, airline passenger

Honor Elizabeth Wainio, 27, Watchung, N.J.
United Flight 93 - Pennsylvania, airline passenger

Gabriela Waisman, 33
World Trade Center

Wendy Wakeford, 40, Freehold, N.J.
World Trade Center

Kenneth Waldie, 46, Methuen, Mass.
American Flight 11 - WTC, airline passenger

Glen J. Wall, 38, Rumson, N.J.
World Trade Center

Peter Wallace, 66, Lincoln Park, N.J.
World Trade Center

Lt. Robert Wallace
World Trade Center

Roy Wallace, 42, Wyckoff, N.J.
World Trade Center

Jean Marie Wallendorf
World Trade Center

Meta Waller, 60, Alexandria, Va.
Pentagon

John Wallice, Huntington, N.Y.
World Trade Center

James Walsh, 36, Scotch Plains, N.J.
World Trade Center

Jeffrey Patrick Walz, 37, Tuckahoe, N.Y.
World Trade Center

Weibin Wang, 41
World Trade Center

Lt. Michael Warchola, 51, Middle Village, N.Y.
World Trade Center

Stephen G. Ward, 33, Gorham, Maine
World Trade Center

Timothy Ward, 38, San Diego, Calif.
United Flight 175 - WTC, airline passenger

Brian G. Warner, 32, Morganville, N.J.
World Trade Center

Charles Waters
World Trade Center

James T. Waters
World Trade Center

Capt. Patrick Waters, 44
World Trade Center

Kenneth Watson
World Trade Center

Michael H. Waye, 38, Morganville, N.J.
World Trade Center

Todd Weaver, 30, New York, N.Y.
World Trade Center

Nathaniel Webb, Jersey City, N.J.
World Trade Center

William Weems, 46, Marblehead, Mass.
United Flight 175 - WTC, airline passenger

Michael Weinberg, 34, New York, N.Y.
World Trade Center

Steven Weinberg, 41, New City, N.Y.
World Trade Center

Simon Weiser, 65
World Trade Center

David Weiss, 41, Maybrook, N.Y.
World Trade Center

David T. Weiss, 50, New York, N.Y.
World Trade Center

Deborah Welsh, 49, New York, N.Y.
United Flight 93 - Pennsylvania, flight crew

Timothy Welty
World Trade Center

John Wenckus, 46, Torrance, Calif.
American Flight 11 - WTC, airline passenger

Oleh D. Wengerchunk
World Trade Center

Peter M. West, 54, Pottersville, N.J.
World Trade Center

Meredith Whale
World Trade Center

firefighter , New York Fire Department
World Trade Center

Adam White
World Trade Center

Edward White
World Trade Center

Staff Sgt. Maudlyn A. White, 38, St. Croix, Virgin
Islands
Pentagon

Sandra L. White, 44, Dumfries, Va.
Pentagon

Leanne Marie Whiteside, 31
World Trade Center

Mark Whitford, 31, Salisbury Mills, N.Y.
World Trade Center

Leslie A. Whittington, 45, University Park, Md.
American Flight 77 - Pentagon, airline passenger

Michael Wholey, Westwood, N.J.
World Trade Center

William J. Wik, 44, Crestwood, N.Y.
World Trade Center

Alison Wildman, 30, New York, N.Y.
World Trade Center

Lt. Glenn Wilkinson, 46, Bayport, N.Y.
World Trade Center

Ernest M. Willcher, 62, North Potomac, Md.
Pentagon

John Willett, 29, New York, N.Y.
World Trade Center

Candace Lee Williams, 20, Danbury, Conn.
American Flight 11 - WTC, airline passenger

Lt. Cmdr. David Lucian Williams, 32, Newport, Ore.
Pentagon

Maj. Dwayne Williams, 40, Jacksonville, Ala.
Pentagon

Kevin Williams
World Trade Center

Lt. John Williamson, 46, Warwick, N.Y.
World Trade Center

Cynthia Wilson, 52, Pelham Bay, N.Y.
World Trade Center

Donna Wilson, 48
World Trade Center

David H. Winton
World Trade Center

Alan Wisniewski, 47, Howell, N.J.
World Trade Center

Frank T. Wisniewski, 54, Basking Ridge, N.J.
World Trade Center

David Wiswall, 54
World Trade Center

Christopher Wodenshek, 35, Hasbrouck Heights, N.J.
World Trade Center

Martin P. Wohlforth, 47, Greenwich, Conn.
World Trade Center

Yin Ping (Steven) Wong, 34
World Trade Center

Brent J. Woodall
World Trade Center

Marvin Woods, 58, Great Mills, Md.
Pentagon

Patrick Woods, 36
World Trade Center

Richard H. Woodwell, 44, Ho-Ho-Kus, N.J.
World Trade Center

Capt. David Wooley
World Trade Center

John B. Works, 36, Darien, Conn.
World Trade Center

Martin M. Wortley, 29, Park Ridge, N.J.
World Trade Center

Rodney J. Wotton, 36, Middletown, N.J.
World Trade Center

John Wright, 33, Rockville Centre, N.Y.
World Trade Center

Neil R. Wright, 30
World Trade Center

Naomi Yajima, 21, Rutherford, N.J.
World Trade Center

Jupiter Yambem, 41, Beacon, N.Y.
World Trade Center

John Yamnicky, 71, Waldorf, Md.
American Flight 77 - Pentagon, airline passenger

Vicki C. Yancey, 43, Springfield, Va.
American Flight 77 - Pentagon, airline passenger

Shuyin Yang, 61, Beijing, China
American Flight 77 - Pentagon, airline passenger,
Chinese

Matthew D. Yarnell, 26, Kinnelon, N.J.
World Trade Center

Myrna Yaskulka
World Trade Center

Kevin Wayne Yokum, 27, Lake Charles, La.
Pentagon

Paul Yoon
World Trade Center

Kevin P. York, 31, Princeton, N.J.
World Trade Center

Raymond York, 45, Valley Stream, N.Y.
World Trade Center

Suzanne Youmans, 60
World Trade Center

Barrington L. Young
World Trade Center

Donald McArthur Young, 41, Roanoke, Va.
Pentagon

Edmond Young, 22, Owings, Md.
Pentagon

Lisa Young, 36, Germantown, Md.
Pentagon

Elkin Yuen, 32
World Trade Center

Joseph Zaccoli, 39, Valley Stream, N.Y.
World Trade Center

Adel A. Zakhary, 50, North Arlington, N.J.
World Trade Center

Arkadi Zaltman, 45
World Trade Center, Moldovan

Robert Zampieri, 30
World Trade Center

Mark Zangrilli, 36, Pompton Plains, N.J.
World Trade Center

Christopher Zarba, 47, Hopkinton, Mass.
American Flight 11 - WTC, airline passenger

Aurelio Zedillo
World Trade Center

Kenneth Zelman, 40, Succasunna, N.J.
World Trade Center

Marc Zeplin
World Trade Center

Yuguang Zheng, 65, Beijing, China
American Flight 77 - Pentagon, airline passenger,
Chinese

Michael J. Zinzi, 37, Newfoundland, N.J.
World Trade Center

Charles A. Zion, 54, Greenwich, Conn.
World Trade Center

Julie L. Zipper, 44, Paramus, N.J.
World Trade Center

Salvatore J. Zisa, 45, Hawthorne, N.J.
World Trade Center

Prokopios Zois, 46, Lynbrook, N.Y.
World Trade Center

And others known only to God.

FREE CD

By

Christine Wyrtzen

Songs to Soothe the Spirit

After reading David's book, you may feel there is no hope for mankind when man can perpetuate such heinous acts. That's why we are proud to present this special CD by Christine Wyrtzen that will warm your soul and soothe your spirit. We are proud to bring it to you FREE of charge (shipping and handling apply). Order one today.

Christine Wyrtzen is the founder and director of Daughters of Promise, a national ministry for women. She is also a recording artist, author, speaker, and host of the nationally syndicated radio program Daughters of Promise, heard daily on over 500 stations. She has performed for over 24 years as a musician with 15 albums and one book to her credit. She's been nominated for a Dove Award and long admired for her ability to communicate to an audience. She is an artist with words, and her poetic bent is evident in whatever she touches.

This CD contains songs form her best-selling album For Those Who Hurt – an encouragement for those who suffer from the hardships of life. You will love her gentle spirit as well as her music.

Order from our website:

www.bookforsale.com

Or call 1-800-765-6691